Gods & Goddesses

Anjula Bedi

ℓESHWAR

About the Author

Anjula Bedi is a freelance writer, and has contributed to several magazines and newspapers. Her short story *Street Tale* was judged the runner-up in the Commonwealth Broadcasting Association, London, Short Story Competition for 1997. She is a script writer for TV, in both Hindi and English, and has also been performing in theatre in both languages. She also works as editor in her publishing company, Eminence Designs Pvt Ltd. She lives and works in Mumbai.

𝑒ESHWAR is an imprint of

BUSINESS PUBLICATIONS INC

A Quartette Group Company

© Anjula Bedi 1998
ISBN 81-86982-04-3
Illustrations by Samir Bagkar
Cover Design by Sunil Mehta, Signatures, Mumbai

Published by
𝑒ESHWAR
229/A, Second Floor, Krantiveer Rajguru Marg,
Girgaon, Mumbai 400004

Contents

Prologue IN MAN'S IMAGE 6

IN THE BEGINNING *The Need For A God* 13

THE *VEDIC* GODS 17

    Indra 18

    Surya 21

    Agni 23

    Vayu 25

    Varuna 26

BRAHMA *The Creator* 27

VISHNU *The Preserver* 33

    Garuda 38

    The Ten Avatars 39

SHIVA *The Destroyer* 59

DEVI *The Mother Goddess* 67

    Durga — The Slayer Of Demons 72

    Kali — The Power Of Time 74

    Annapoorna — The Giver Of Plenty 75

CONSORTS OF THE GODS *The Female Triad* 77

    Saraswati — The Muse 79

    Lakshmi — The Beautiful 82

    Parvati — The Gentle One 85

SONS OF THE GODS 89

    Ganesha — The Wise One 90

    Kartikeya — The Warrior 94

    Hanuman — The Faithful 97

ALL THINGS HOLY 101

Epilogue THE UNDEFINABLE 108

Writer's Note

 These were fairy tales, the stories of gods and goddesses – to which I listened in fascination from grandmothers and aunts, and even the women who worked in the household and were very much a part of the family. They were essentially the same stories, but each version differed a little from the other, and each narrator added a new and charming character to the known story, which in turn led to heated denials and arguments amongst the knowledgable. But for the listener, it was a wonder that each god or goddess was associated with every story and appeared in one form or the other. These stories made me think of this magical being, God, Iswar, Parmatma, who was everywhere and in everything and yet could not be seen except in our imagination. He was Brahma, he was Saraswati, he was Ganesha or Hanuman. He was a tree in the backyard or a stone placed under it; he was the sun that rose in the morning, the moon, and even the river that one dipped in at Hardwar or Benaras.

The stories associated with each god and goddess remained in my subconscious and that they can still be recalled after four decades of disruption and rootlessness proves that they have withstood the test of time... as indeed they have, almost 4000 years in time.

Of course, this account barely touches the tip of the wealth of literature and belief that has grown round the Hindu pantheon, for to understand and even claim to know a part of the four *Vedas*, the 18 *Puranas*, and the two epics, the *Ramayana* and the *Mahabharata*, one would have to take a thousand rebirths and reincarnations. But since the goal of Hindu thought is *moksha* or salvation through *jnana* or knowledge, we will keep striving towards it.

I am deeply grateful to both my grandmother (one, who at 95 is still a great source of information), who recounted these stories in such an inimitable manner so as to kindle an academic interest in the meaning of these colourful parables, and to my father who, having a childlike fascination for these tales, attempted all his life to explain to me the link between the *avatars*, worship and modern cosmology.

I marvel at the patience and knowledge of my cousin, Rita, who having heard the stories from the same grandmother, interpreted and applied them better, thus painstakingly keying in, editing and correcting the manuscript, despite several technical hitches. My husband Satish, being a compulsive book-buyer, helped unwittingly by supplying several of the books needed for reference.

I thank Chandralekha Maitra for giving me the opportunity to compile stories remembered from times past, for the present.

Last but not least, I pay obeisance to Vishvakarma, the divine architect for the gift of the word processor which has enabled me to update my own knowledge and provided a tool, which as a writer I shall henceforth hold sacred.

Prologue
In Man's Image

What form His devotees desire, that form itself the Lord takes;
What name His devotees desire, that name itself the Lord takes;
In what manner the devotees desire Him
And stand thinking of Him with unwinking eyes,
In that manner itself does the Lord of the Discus present Himself.

Saint-poet Poihai

The gods were all gathered, prostrating themselves before Vishnu, begging him to give them something which would protect them from the powers of evil, the *asuras* or *daityas*. Brahma was there, and Surya, Shiva, Agni, Yama (the God of Death), Varuna and all the tribes of the immortals we now worship. But at that time they were not invulnerable. They invoked Vishnu, the Indefinable. And Vishnu was in all of them – 'this assembly of divinities that now has come before thee, thou art' – one God but manifested in so many forms.

Vishnu advised them to cast all the medicinal herbs into the ocean of milk and churn it to produce the *amrit* or ambrosia which would make them immortal. And the gods did so and attained immortality. Ever since, Man has been striving towards something beyond this existence. *Moksha*, salvation, immortality, call it what you will, it is an attainable prospect but it requires a medium, a god like Vishnu, who can assist mortals to achieve this goal, which is perceived as a union with the Supreme Spirit.

Each religion prescribes different paths to salvation, recorded in their scriptures. The goal of Hindu thought is *moksha* through knowledge, knowledge of the self, towards self-realisation. This is the way of the *yogi*, who has recognised the Supreme Spirit within himself and for whom there is no need for an intermediary. But not everyone could aspire towards knowledge, so the stepping stone in the first stage of spiritual development was the image of God, the *pratima* or reflection of the godhead. The image became a reflection of the abstract principle which the common man was unable to comprehend. The believer was apprehensive and in awe of the unseen, mental image of a god and was more comfortable with the seen, no matter how terrifying the image, like the one of the Goddess Kali.

Though Hindu metaphysical thought propagates a belief in one God, over the centuries religious thinkers concretised the idea of God in metaphors from daily life, and an entire pantheon of gods was conceived, representing various aspects of life. In fact, it is believed that there are 86 crore gods and goddesses in the Hindu pantheon, making it a little short of one god to each person of the 90 crore population.

Hindu worship acknowledges several gods, since all forms and manifestations are aspects of divinity. The poet Basavanna, writing in the 12th century AD, had put it very simply, "The pot is God, the winnowing fan is God; the stone in the street is God, the comb is God. The bowstring is also a god. The bushel is a god and the spouted cup is a god." The eternal truths taught by the *Upanishads* were too complex for the common mind. The majority of the people were not literate, but had the benefit of faith and belief through which they participated in the learning process. It was through the stories of the *Puranas* (the 'old' stories), 18 in number, and through the two great epics, the *Ramayana* and the *Mahabharata*, that their religious beliefs were imparted to them. There were stories within stories, all of symbolic significance and through these their *dharma* or way of life was explained to them, with divinity being brought to their level. Thus the gods were born, grew up, quarrelled, cursed, married and had children, in fact, did everything that mortals did. And as such, they too were bound by *karma* and no one was above reward and punishment. The gods were pleased by the attention and love of their devotees and offended by neglect. But like benevolent elders, they could be propitiated by prayers and penance. And no one, whether celestial being, demon or human, was beyond their sphere of influence. So Brahma, the Creator, pleased with the devotion of Ravana, the demon king of Lanka, granted him a boon that made him invulnerable to gods and demons alike. Another evil king, Hiranyakashyapa, obtained the sovereignty of the three *lokas* (worlds) through his austerities and penance.

One of the greatest assets of the Hindu religion brought out by these stories was its liberality, since the gods gave a fair chance to all to repent and make amends for past sins. It is said in the *Satapatha Brahmana*, a part of the *Vedas*, that there was a time when both gods and demons were equal and were the progeny of Prajapati, the creator. They were all mortal, but looked for ways and means to attain immortality. Then Prajapati taught the gods a sacrifice which would make them immortal. But the sacrifice was not enough; to gain superiority over the demons, they had to become truthful and forego falsehood. So the gods became immortal and greater than the demons by following the path of sacrifice and truth, while the demons became weaker since they depended increasingly on untruth. According to this story, there was only a fine line that separated the mortal from the immortal – the precarious path of truth.

The similarities between Man and the anthropomorphic representations of God were so pronounced that it was easy to identify with them. One could believe that they were human but had evolved into gods through the acquisition of knowledge, as Krishna in the *Mahabharata*. It gave each mortal the faith that he could aspire to the godhead. Thus, in this process of evolution, man begins with the worship of the more manifest forms of divinity to understand the transcendental being; he goes from the visible to the invisible.

To the Hindu, the Universe is his temple and so every object in it has a divine nature. The *Vishnu Purana* says that God is one, 'in whom are all things; from whom are all things'. If the Universe is a divine creation then there is nothing in it that is not divine, and no form of worship that is false. As God created, preserved, protected and destroyed, he wielded influence on every aspect of human existence; so there had to be as many gods as there were aspects of life. The *Vedas*, the first known religious texts, gave detailed descriptions of the deities of nature and the eleménts but there was no emphasis on images. '*Om* is God; *Om* is all', say the *Vedas* and from this sacred word all things began.

Inspired by the detailed description in the *Vedas*, sculptors fashioned images with the attributes described in the texts. Soon these images became the objects of worship in the home or in temples for public worship. And yet the temple is only of secondary importance, for Hindus in essence believe in individual worship in which the worshipper has a direct and intimate relationship with his God, without an intermediary. He prostrates himself before the image to subjugate his ego to his God and sits before Him in meditation, offering flowers and incense as a prelude to complete concentration. The eyes of a Hindu image are prominent features to foster this intimate relationship. The image is installed in a separate *puja* (prayer) room like a guest. The 'guest' is woken up in the morning with tinkling bells, bathed, dressed in different *vastras* (garments), offered floral and edible offerings and left in isolation while he blesses this *prasad* by partaking of it. This is then distributed among all the members of the household. He is then laid in bed till it is time for the evening *aarti* (worship with an oil lamp) when the whole family gets together to thank God for the blessings of the day. The installation of an image in the house performs a social function too. Since God is always in your house, watching your every action, right living is essential. Purity, honesty, serenity, your *dharma* (the right way of life) have to be observed to show respect towards the deity. In times of need, he is your saviour and if your faith and belief are strong, you are the recipient of his favours. H.A. Rose in *Hindu Gods and Goddesses* says, 'The evils the Hindus feared from their gods were physical; the help they looked for was material, not spiritual'. Material gain was not looked down upon and is worshipped symbolically in the form of Lakshmi, the Goddess of Fortune.

Aspects of Nature and manifestations of physical forces are deified and each is allotted a god. Every man or woman has complete freedom to choose his or her own *ishta devta* or personal God. But the Hindu has always been flexible and ready to accept other gods he encountered into his realm of worship, and the Hindu gods do not seem to object. Besides belief in the gods of the Hindu pantheon, he is not averse to including gods and saints from other religions too. It is not unusual to see a *puja* room replete not only with Hindu gods and goddesses, but pictures and symbols of the Buddha, Christ, the Sufi saints or Guru Nanak, since no Hindu can negate a divine form without apprehensions of its effect on him and his family. This multiple approach towards worship is perhaps responsible for the preservation and survival of this religion despite invasions and onslaughts from other religious groups. It has removed all the dos and don'ts that would be obstacles to the path of knowledge and discovery. Since Hinduism was not founded on a revelation, and did not have a central figure who was the teacher or prophet, it is believed that the whole truth may never have been revealed and each believer may still experience new revelations in his individual worship. Each image of worship is *sampoorna*, that is, complete in itself and each deity teaches us something. Hence he is *sarthak*, meaningful, rather than *nirarthak*, without meaning.

It is said that the image in the Hindu religion is like a diagram to a geometrician; it provides a focus for his thoughts and worship. In fact, the scriptures have advocated image worship mainly for the unevolved, before they slowly graduate to the transcendent. Image worship cannot be an end in itself, and cannot free one from the cycle of birth and rebirth. The union of the soul can be achieved only through knowledge and non-attachment to material things. Every stage of life has been symbolised by a deity – Krishna, the child and lover; Hanuman, the bachelor; Rama, the husband and ideal ruler; Shiva, the ascetic; Yama, the God of Death. Human aspirations too are deified – Lakshmi, the Goddess of Fortune; Saraswati, the Goddess of Learning and the fine arts; Parvati, the gentle mother; Durga, the victor; Kubera, the God of Wealth; Kama and Rati, the God and Goddess of Love; Varuni, the Goddess of Wine; Sashti, Goddess of Childbirth, protector of children; even diplomacy has a god – Narada. Yet the scriptures still reiterate, 'the real divinity is one; the virtuous have given it many a name'.

The religion itself is very practical and has no ethical doctrines. Thus Hindus worship not only the positive aspects of God, which in any case are favourable, but even the negative attributes, to propitiate the gods and goddesses and thus keep evil at bay. The religion could not ignore the interaction between the male and the female, since they were the symbols of creation, one of the first acts of God. So sexual love, marriage, incest and adultery were all dealt with in the legends about the gods. Like mortals, gods too had the potential for good and evil. Angered by acts of omission, they would send famine and pestilence to the world. But the evil was always balanced by an act of divine grace. Indra, the god of rain, jealous of the devotion of the people of Gokul and Vrindavan for the cowherd, Krishna, an incarnation of Vishnu the Preserver, sent a deluge to the land and unwittingly provided an opportunity to Krishna to display his supernatural powers. Krishna is said to have lifted the mountain, Govardhan, in his hand and gathered all his devotees under it. There are several such examples of this tussle between the gods, but basically most of the stories deal with gods and demons and the victory of good over evil. The Hindu worshipper abandoned ritual and sacrifice, which had brought about the dominance of the Brahmin priests, and turned to *bhakti* or devotionalism, which advocated complete surrender and love for the *ishta devta*. The Hindus were aware that the images were symbols and not actual living entities, but God was now seen as the beloved who was wooed through beautiful devotional poetry and *kirtans* (devotional songs) which evoked ecstatic responses in the devotees. God seemed within reach and the idea of a union with the beloved appeared to be the simplest way of explaining Man's relationship with God. Divinity too, seemed to adapt itself to this new concept, and the deity only revealed his gentler aspects. But Man's restlessness never gives up the search for the *Brahman* or Supreme Spirit. As Kabir, one of the medieval *bhakti* poets, writes,

Just as the deer searches for musk in the forest
Though carrying it in his navel
So does the world search for Rama
Forgetting that He resides in everyone and everything.

In The Beginning

The Need For A God

इयं विसृष्टिर्यत आबभूव यदिं वा दधे
यदि वा त
यो अस्याध्यक्ष : परमे व्योमन् त्सो अंङ्ग
वेद यदि वा त वेद

By whom were the mighty earth and heaven made firm,
By whom was the vault of heaven made fast...
To what God should we do homage with our oblation ?

~ Rig Veda

Long, long ago, was it 5000 years ago... but perhaps time is not of consequence, for Time has not played a part in this drama of Hindu existence. There was an existence prior to the present and there will always be an existence in this cycle of birth and rebirth, of incarnation and reincarnation. The world was not created, it was *anadi* (without a beginning), its creation already existed in a Timelessness, perceived only by the Supreme Being, who manifested Himself in countless forms. For, as the *Chandayoga Upanishad* says, 'How could Being be produced from Non-Being?' But there was a restlessness in Man's mind which made him search not only for fresher pastures and newer forms of settlement but also for newer aspects of God. So it was that almost 5000 years ago, in this manifestation of the world of *maya* (illusion) which we perceive as the real world, the first gods made themselves known to man.

The history of what are now known as the Hindu gods, goes back to the early Dravidians, the original settlers and descendants of the Proto-Dravidians who came to India between 4000 to 2500 BC. Indian mythology had its beginnings at that time and remarkably, it is still part of a living culture, followed by people from all walks of life and having a homogeneity in the whole of the Hindu world. Being agricultural, the Dravidians' gods were all connected with fertility – the phallic symbol, found on the seals at Harappa in the Indus Valley or

the goddess out of whose womb grow plants and trees. Surrounding these figures are animals, some real, like the bull, elephant, deer, tiger or rhinoceros, and some mythical – half-ram and half-bull. There were serpents too, which later form strong associations with current Hindu deities like Shiva, Ganesha and Vishnu. Was the seed of later Hinduism already sown in these representations of God – Shiva, the phallic symbol; Devi, the Mother Goddess, the fount of all regeneration?

Perhaps it was, but there was one important event in the history of India which ensured this continuity and formed the link between its Dravidian past and the present.

Around 1700 BC, came a new invasion, unsettling and destroying the quiet, undisturbed life of the Indus Valley. The Aryans, tall, white-skinned and fond of the good life, descended with horses, chariots and swords, completely overshadowing the peaceful Dravidians with their nomadic lifestyle.

They brought with them their own deities, representing the elements and the natural phenomena. They deified heroism and war and contemptuously referred to the Dravidians as *dasyus* or slaves. But they gave to the world a brilliant collection of hymns, the *Vedas*, which were originally said to have been breathed by God himself, a direct gift of God to Man. These are four in number, beginning with the *Rig Veda*, then the *Yajur Veda*, *Sama Veda* and *Atharva Veda*.The word *Veda* comes from the root *vid*, which means 'to know', hence the *Vedas* signify knowledge. Indeed, it is from the *Vedas* that we get our knowledge of the Vedic deities, many of whom are precursors of the known Hindu gods. The term 'Hindu' is derived from the Persian word 'Sindhu', the Sanskrit name for the river Indus, and must have come into existence in the 6th century BC when the territory round the Indus formed part of the Persian Empire. The name seems to have disappeared with the exit of the Persians, but came back again with the Muslim invasion from the north-west, though at that time it did not have any religious connotation. It first assumed a religious tint during the British Raj. Thus, the religion itself seems to have evolved from a combination of the faiths of the original inhabitants and the Aryan invaders. Though the conquerors proclaimed the superiority of a cruder form of religion over the age-old wisdom of the land, they subsequently came under the spell of the religious beliefs of the Dravidians and amalgamated them within their own fold.

So the link remained, but a whole new pantheon of gods was added, which has evolved over the centuries to give us what is seen as the modern Hindu polytheism, so much so, that it is now difficult to imagine that there were once two distinct systems.

The early Aryan gods, the Vedic gods, were deifications of natural forces – *Agni* (Fire), *Varuna* (Waves), *Vayu* (Wind), *Indra* (Sky) and *Surya* (Sun). Their attributes were so minutely described in the *Vedas*, that though there were no images of them, they took on human forms in the imaginations of the devotees. The Aryans preferred abstract principles incorporated in the *Rig Veda* which called for ritual sacrifice, *homa* (the ritual fire), as the only form of worship.

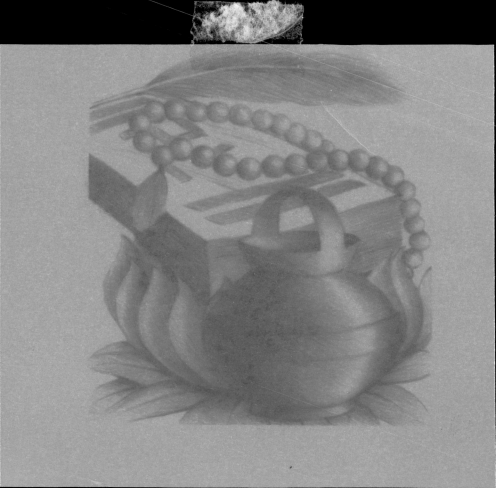

The Vedic Gods

ॐ भूर्भुव : स्व : तत्सविदुर्वरे व्यम् ।
भर्गो देवस्य धीमहि धियो यो तः
प्रचोदयात

Indra

Friend Indra, from thy sky descend
Thy course propitious hither bend.

~ Rig Veda

Gods and men were in a turmoil when the serpent Vritra had trapped the world's water by coiling himself round the reservoirs. There was drought on earth and men prayed to the gods to protect them, and in answer to their prayers, Indra was born. Soon after his birth, he snatched the mace, *Vajra*, from his father and went forth to attack Vritra, the demon of drought. But before he ventured forth, he was given offerings of *soma*, the intoxicating juice which fortified and strengthened him. Vritra was struck and killed by the thunderbolt *Vajra* and Indra broke open the mountains releasing torrents of water on to the parched earth. The Indra-Vitra confrontation is linked to the Vedic creation myth. Indra's victory releases the waters, thus rejuvenating the world. Even to this day, Indra's name is invoked to end droughts. It is said that after every summer he throws out his thunderbolt and brings rain, reminding people of his might. Indra, the most prominent god in the *Rig Veda*, is identified as the Storm God, or the Rain God, whose popularity is assured in India's hot, dry climate. His thunderbolt, *Vajra*, and the bow, *Indradhanush*, protect mankind from the vagaries of nature, symbolised in the *asuras* (the demons). Thus, he is both revered as the God of Rain, and feared as the God of Storms. He represents the electrical energy brought to earth by the rain, rejuvenating it and making it fertile. He is sometimes seen as a fertility god.

He is said to be ever-young and has all the qualities of youth; he is impulsive, heroic and exuberant. He is the force out of which all power is born, and he is the embodiment of service to the gods and men. His life is dedicated to defending men and animals against the evil designs of the demons. The tales of his wars with the *asuras* are legion. Asura Virochana defeated him and gained supremacy over the three *lokas* or worlds. The god Vishnu came to his aid and took the Vamana (dwarf) *avatar* and with his three gigantic steps, claimed the whole world again for Indra. The gods often appealed to him to send his thunderbolt to destroy demons like Ravana's brother, Kumbhakarana, in the *Ramayana*. But he seems to be insecure in his kingdom of Amravati, the Celestial City, near Mount Meru, the abode of Brahma. For he is ever-watchful of the sages who offer prayers and penance, hoping for salvation and power through their meditations. He sends celestial maidens to seduce them so that their prayers would lose their efficacy. He himself is said to have seduced Ahalya, the wife of the sage Gautama. For this affront, Gautama cursed him and condemned him to having a thousand impressions of the female organ all over his body. Later, through prayers and penance, these were converted into a thousand eyes.

Indra drew Brahma's wrath upon himself and was defeated by Ravana's son Meghnath. To rescue him the gods had to grant Meghnath the conditional boon of immortality.

The Aryan invaders sought help from various gods, specially Indra, who was the manifestation of vitality and creative energy. He was the warrior who could help them against the obstructive forces of the native Dravidians. In the *Vedas*, he is the Aryan warrior-king, handsome and fair complexioned. He rides a horse, or more often a chariot drawn by several horses, with Vayu, God of the Wind, as his charioteer. Like the kings, he is fond of *soma* (wine) which gives him the strength to go into battle.

The Vedic image of Indra is that of a man with four arms. With two hands he holds a lance, in the third his thunderbolt, and the fourth is empty. His mount is the celestial elephant Airvarta. Indra soon replaced Vishnu in the Vedic Trinity, thus symbolising the later caste struggle, the Brahmins or teachers pitted against the Kshatriyas or warriors. Varuna, the God of the Ocean, was the chief of the gods but Indra replaced him in the same way as in later Hinduism Brahma was dominated by Vishnu and his *avatars*.

In the *Puranic* tales, Indra and Krishna (a reincarnation of Vishnu) appear to be rivals. Before Krishna's advent as a cowherd, Indra had been the god of the pastoral people. Krishna's miracles and strength turned them towards his worship. Indra was furious and sent a deluge which threatened to submerge the area. Krishna lifted up the mountain of Govardhan on one finger, providing an umbrella for the people for seven days, after which Indra had to acknowledge his supremacy. The *Vishnu Purana* relates another story of the conflict between Indra and Krishna. Once, when Krishna and his wife Satyabhama went to visit Indra, Satyabhama saw the *parijat* tree planted in Indra's garden. This tree had emerged with the churning of the ocean and had been claimed by Indra. At Satyabhama's request, Krishna carried the tree to his vehicle, Garuda. Incensed, Indra threw his thunderbolt at him, but Krishna caught it comfortably in his hand and carrying away the tree planted it in his garden. Once again Indra had been defeated by Krishna.

Swarga or heaven, aspired to by most Hindus, is Indra's domain, where the good go for a short while as they wait for their turn to be reincarnated. And this carries on till the soul has completed its cycle of rebirths and can become one with the Supreme Being.

Indra is still worshipped annually in Bengal and his image is immersed in the waters the next day to propitiate the Gods and stem the fury of the rains.

Inspite of his powerful arsenal of weapons, Indra, Lord of the Sky, is a peaceful, heavenly ruler who offers refuge to all those who seek him and follow the path of *dharma*.

Surya

We meditate on that excellent light of that divine Sun :
May He illuminate our minds.
~ Vishnu Purana

 The sun, *Surya*, is referred to as a *devta* (god) by all Hindus and life begins with its rise and ends when it sets. The hymn to the sun, the *Gayatri mantra*, is considered the holiest verse of the *Vedas* and was supposed to be whispered into the ears of a male child at birth so that no profane ears could hear it. So afraid were the translators of the *Vedas* of contaminating it, that they refrained from translating it! The *Skanda Purana* says that nothing in the *Vedas* is superior to the *Gayatri* and by repeating it, a man can redeem himself.

The *Gayatri* is the link between the Vedic and the post-Vedic Surya. In the *Vedas*, Surya is the eighth son of Aditi (Infinity), who had cast him away. The eight sons were supposed to be the eight spheres of existence. Surya's wife is Usha (Dawn), but in the *Ramayana*, he is called the son of Aditi and Kashyapa and also the son of Brahma, the Creator. In this story, his wife is Sanjana, the daughter of the architect of the gods, Vishwakarma. Sanjana was so dazzled by her husband's radiance that she could not live with him and left him, substituting Chayya (Shadow) for herself. Surya lived with Chayya for years without discovering the truth, and it was only when Chayya cursed Sanjana's child and the curse took immediate effect that Surya realised that she was not the child's mother, nor his wife. His prayers revealed Sanjana's hiding place in the forest and he lived with her for some time, she as a mare and he as a horse. When they returned, his father-in-law Vishwakarma, cut off one-eighth of his brightness so that his daughter Sanjana could live in peace. With these parts which were taken off, he fashioned Vishnu's mace and Shiva's trident, besides other weapons of the gods. In the *Mahabharata*, he is named as the father of Karna. Kunti wished to have a son by Surya, because of a boon given her by Sage Durvasa. Surya, being the repository of energy, power and radiance, is also the sustainer of life. He is represented in the *Vedas* as a handsome man, riding a chariot of light, drawn by seven horses, representing each day of the week. In the *Puranas* he is described as a red man with three eyes and four arms, two arms bearing water-lilies, while the other two are in the *varada mudra* or gesture of bestowing blessings and encouraging his worshippers. He sits on a red lotus while rays of brightness emanate from his body.

Later, in the post-Vedic age, the sun was seen as the precursor of the Trinity – the concept of God as Creator, Preserver and Destroyer. He represents the cycle of birth, life and death, fertilising the earth with his warmth and giving new life. His energy preserves life and his heat burns everything in the end.

There are three important shrines to Surya, one in Modhera in Gujarat, one in Martand in Kashmir, and of course the most famous, Konarak in Orissa, all of them over a thousand years old. But Surya does not need any images, for he is seen every day by his worshippers, galloping across the sky, while they offer the *surya-namaskar* to him, thanking him for his generosity, which prompts him to give everything of himself without asking for anything in return. He is golden-eyed and golden-tongued, a benevolent god who moves according to fixed laws, thereby granting stability to the world. His symbol is the *swastika*.

He distributes energy to gods, men, animals and plants, since he is said to be the original source of *amrit* (nectar) which he passes on to the moon for distribution in the Universe.

Agni

O Agni, be easy of access to us as a father to his son
Join us for our well-being.

~ Rig Veda

 Agni, the God of Fire, resides in every home and is linked to a household priest. He is immortal, but has made all homes his abode since he is the protector of all ceremonies and helps men to perform their sacrifices in the correct way. He flits swiftly between heaven and earth, carrying man's oblations to God and accompanying the gods to the place of sacrifice. In other words, he forms the liaison between the worshipper and the worshipped. He is the personification of the sacrificial fire around which Vedic religion developed.

The discovery of fire was a very important landmark in the history of civilisation and Man was in awe of this strange flame. It was natural that all kinds of myths and stories grew around this almost supernatural phenomenon. The Aryans developed the worship of fire to an extraordinary degree, and the highest divine functions were ascribed to Agni. He is said to be the son of heaven and earth; in the *Vishnu Purana* he is said to be the son of Brahma, the Creator.

His strength was so great that only he could carry Shiva's seed over the ocean and create his son Kartikeya.

Agni is invoked to be a witness to all significant events. Hindu homes have the *havan, home* or sacrificial fire, for important occasions, be it a naming ceremony, the sacred thread ceremony, or marriage, each an important event in an individual's life. The body at death too, has to be placed on the sacrificial pyre, and Agni is asked to warm the mortal part before carrying it to the world of the righteous. Sita, in the *Ramayana*, to prove her chastity after having been abducted by Ravana, goes through the *agni pariksha* (ordeal by fire).

According to a Vedic hymn, Agni has three forms, as fire on earth, as lightning in the atmosphere and as the golden sun in heaven. The light and warmth of Agni bring joy into every home because he dispels the terrors of darkness that plague humankind. He infuses confidence in his worshippers and even the powers of evil seem to be reduced by his spark. He brings wealth, prosperity and longevity to his devotees. Because of its omnipresence, all things, including earth and heaven, obey his commands.

In the *Mahabharata*, Agni is said to have exhausted his vigour because of his over-indulgence in sacrifice.

In the eternal fight between good and evil Agni was called upon by the gods to destroy the Kravyads, flesh-eating *rakshasas*, even though he himself consumes flesh. He took the form of a Kravyad with iron tusks and charged the *rakshasas*, killing them with his tusks and then consuming them.

The worship of Agni on earth was established by the Bhrigus, priests descended from the sage Bhrigu, who had received the gift of fire through a celestial being, Matarisvana.

The image of Agni is that of a red man with three flaming heads, three legs and seven arms, wearing a garland of fruit and riding a ram. The three legs represent the three fires – the ceremonial , the nuptial and the sacrificial; they could also denote the three worlds or *lokas* over which he has power, the celestial, the terrestrial and the infernal. The Vedic Agni becomes Rudra or Shiva, the Destroyer, in the Puranic period.

Agni found a place in all the pantheons because of the role he plays in all sacrifices which even today form an important part of Hindu ritual.

Vayu

Touching the sky, he moves onwards making all things ruddy ;
And he comes propelling the dust of the earth.

~ Rig Veda

 This is *Vayu*, the God of the Winds, who rules over the atmosphere. After Indra, he is perhaps the most prominent of the storm gods of the *Vedas* and is often associated with him. He is presented as riding the golden chariot of Indra, pulled by anything from 99 to a 1000 horses, red or purple in colour. Since he is supposed to have been born from the breath of Purusa, the Supreme Being, he is God of the Wind.

He is supposed to infuse the Universe with life, and to purify the atmosphere as Pavan (the pure) and it is said that his sounds have been heard but his form has never been seen.

Praises have been sung of his swiftness and agility, and later, in the *Ramayana* and the *Mahabharata*, he is said to be the father of two of the strongest and bravest heroes, Hanuman and Bheema respectively. Hanuman is often referred to as Pavanputra, the son of Pavan (Wind) by a monkey mother. Kunti, the mother of Bheema, was permitted to bear a child by any of the gods, since her husband could not become a father due to a curse. The fact that she chose Vayu, points to the fact that his position among the gods must have been significant.

Being associated with purification, he is dressed in white and even carries a white flag. He is often referred to as Maruti, the air necessary for life, or Anila, breath of life.

Varuna

He is the sovereign ruler of the Universe, King of Gods and men.

~ Rig Veda

This God of the Waves is said to dwell in a house with a 1000 doors so that he is always accessible to men. In the *Vedas* he is more powerful than all the other gods because he is said to be the creator and sustainer of the universe and the administrator of the cosmic law. Day and night appear at his bidding and rivers are channelised according to his plans. Varuna is supposed to avenge sin and falsehood and his eye is the sun which keeps a watch on all mortals. In his hand he carries a rope to bind sinners with, symbolic of man being fettered by his sins. He is depicted as four-faced, with a 1000 eyes, is the colour of snow and appears wearing a golden mantle.

In the *Mahabharata*, he is the lord of the waves and of rivers, god of fluidity and movement. He is significant also because he was present at the birth of Arjuna and presented him with his bow, Gandive, with which Arjuna won the battle against the Kauravas. According to the *Puranas* he is said to have carried away Bhadra, the wife of the sage Utathya, whose curse caused Varuna's abodes, the oceans and rivers, to dry up. Thus the god was forced to return Bhadra to her husband, who then allowed the waters to flow again, but Varuna was forced to forego his prominence and one does not find any new images of him.

But since his abode is Pushpagiri, the underwater mountain, he is the protector of fisherfolk, who still invoke him when they go out on to the high seas. Being the god of the rivers, he is also propitiated in times of drought.

Brahma

The Creator

गुरू ब्रह्मा गुरूर्विष्णु: महेश्वर :।
गुरू : साक्षात् परब्रह्म तस्मै श्री गुरवे नम : ॥

 The story of creation begins with Brahma. It is said that the Supreme Being, feeling a vast void around him, was lonely and so he created the water in which he planted a seed. This seed became a golden egg, the Hiranyagarbha, from which after a 1000 years, the Supreme Being manifested himself as Brahma. This egg contained the mighty oceans, the continents, seas and mountains, as well as the gods, demons and mankind; in fact, all forms in existence.

Another legend (in the *Satapatha Upanishad*) says that Brahma is *Swayambhu* or self-existent; he had no beginning and no end. Brahma and the gods rose out of the waters before the creation of the world as it is now. From him descended all the *rishis* (sages). According to the *Mahabharata*, since creation and preservation are so closely linked, Brahma emerged sitting on a lotus that sprang from Vishnu's navel.

The older part of the *Mahabharata* describes him as the original deity from whom all the world is born. He is the all-inclusive Being 'the Source of the Universe, presiding over all Creation, preserving like Vishnu, destroying like Shiva' (*Markandya Purana*).

The name Brahma is not found in the *Vedas* since here the active creator is only the golden egg, Hiranyagarbha. But interestingly, in the Buddhist tales, there is mention of Brahma ruling over the second and third heavenly spheres.

In later Hinduism his position is taken over by Vishnu, the Preserver, who supercedes him in worship, and all Brahma's powers are attributed to Shakti, the female principle. It is as the feminine form of Shakti that Brahma remains the chief object of worship among the Hindus, though he is the masculine form of Immensity.

It is said that after producing 10 sons, his body split into two parts, a male and a female. The female was a beautiful woman called Satrupa. Brahma himself was drawn to her though she was his daughter, and could not take his eyes off her. Each time she moved around him to escape his amorous glances, a new head sprang out of his body so that his eyes could follow her, giving him a total of five heads.

The fifth head of Brahma was destroyed by Shiva to punish Brahma for his arrogance, resulting in the four-headed Brahma that we know today. The Puranic story recounts how Brahma was once asked by the sages to explain the true nature of the godhead. Brahma, influenced by the demon Mahishasura, arrogantly declared that he was the greatest. This led to a dispute between Brahma and Vishnu, who was also present at the gathering. Deciding to take the matter to the *Vedas*, they were surprised when the *Vedas* declared that Shiva was the Supreme Being. Brahma's anger knew no bounds and he challenged the supremacy of Shiva. Shiva, taking the destructive form of Bhairava, cut off Brahma's fifth head with the thumb of his left hand.

According to the *Mahabharata*, Shiva cut off Brahma's head to punish him for his incestuous relationship with his daughter, Satrupa. Another legend says that Brahma's fifth head was the head of a donkey. When the gods defeated the demons in battle, they retreated to the nether world. The donkey's head, turning traitor, admonished the demons and told them that he would help them. This infuriated the gods who asked Vishnu to cut off Brahma's head. Vishnu was hesitant and said that the falling head would destroy the earth. The gods then appealed to Shiva, the destroyer, who bore Brahma to Rudratirath and then cut off his head.

So Brahma is now represented as a four-headed man, red in colour. He is dressed in white and rides a goose. In one hand he carries a staff and in the other a bowl for alms. Sometimes Brahma is represented with four arms in which he carries the four *Vedas*, or he may hold the *Vedas* in one hand while the other hands hold a sceptre, a ritual alms bowl, a string of beads and his bow Parivirta.

He is sometimes depicted as an old man, mature and bearded and riding a swan, a symbol of knowledge. He is also shown standing in a lotus emerging from Vishnu's naval. He lives in Brahmanda, or the Universe. Brahma's abode, Mount Meru, is in the centre of the world, which according to Hindu mythology, is shaped like a wheel.

This is Brahma's heaven, where the river Ganga also has its origin. Around Mount Meru are the cities of the other deities such as Indra, god of the firmament. According to the *Mahabharata*, Brahma's heaven is 800 miles long, 400 miles wide and 40 miles high. Narada, the wandering ascetic, says that even if he extolled its virtues for 200 years, he could not describe its magnificence

Hindu metaphysics believes in three *gunas* or fundamental qualities – *tamas*, the disintegrating tendency; *rajas*, from which all creative impulse springs, and *sattva*, standing for cohesion, purity and devotion. Brahma, being the creative principle, represents the *rajas guna* from which all creativity emanates. He is the universal intellect, the thought process from which the universe rises. Thus he is said to have produced 10 mind-born sons, including the sages Vashishta and Narada. Not only does mental activity start from him but all the qualities existing in god and man also were born of him. *Dharma* or righteousness, was born from his chest, *kama* or desire from his heart, *krodha*, anger from his eyebrows, *lobha* or avarice from his lips, *moha*, involvement from his intellect, *mada*, intoxication from his egoism and *mrtya* or death, from his eyes.

From the powers of his mind Brahma created four types of beings. Out of his thighs came

the demons and *asuras*, from his mouth, the gods and *devtas*, and from his sides the ancestors or *pitri*. Last of all came the humans, born out of his body which split into the male and the female.

When Brahma awakes, the three worlds, heaven, earth and the nether world are created, and when he sleeps, there is chaos. All beings who have not attained *moksha* (liberation from the cycle of birth and death), have to prepare for rebirth when Brahma creates the world again.

There is evidence of sects devoted to Brahma in the 4th century BC. But it is believed that since the task of creation has been accomplished and Brahma's work is over, he has become one with the cosmic principle. Thus Brahma is not generally worshipped. Man and his Universe have been created, now he must look towards the gods who are the protectors and propitiate the one who has the power to destroy.

Yet Brahma's name appears in all the rituals and he has not been forgotten by celestial beings and the seers who are concerned about the management of the Universe.

The image of Brahma is present in most temples but the only famous temple where he is still worshipped is at Pushkar, near Ajmer in Rajasthan.

The *Skanda Purana* gives another reason why Brahma was condemned not to be worshipped. He was cursed by Shiva because he told an untruth. Shiva had manifested himself as a *linga* (phallic symbol) of light and he challenged the gods to find the two ends of this all-pervading, infinite light. Brahma, since he wished to be victorious and considered himself the Supreme Being, pretended that he had found one end. Shiva condemned him to oblivion.

There are some areas of Punjab and Himachal Pradesh where traces of Brahma worship are still found. In a temple at Dera in Kulu, prayers are said to the Adi Brahma during Baisakh (April) and Sawan (June-July).

It is said that a villager in Kulu once saw a Brahmin sitting in a lonely spot. When asked who he was, the Brahmin said that he was God, and if people built a temple to him at that spot and worshipped him there, their wishes would be granted. So saying, he disappeared beneath the earth and the people of the village built a temple where they installed an image of black stone. In many parts of Haryana and Punjab, a stone is placed under a banyan tree and worshipped as Brahma, in the hope of being cured of fevers and for help in recovering lost property. The rivalry between Shiva and Brahma manifested itself in many stories. It was the conflict of the opposing forces, the creator and the destroyer, with each one trying to prove his supremacy. It is interesting to note that Shiva was able to banish Brahma, who according to some stories was also the father of Shiva in his incarnation as Rudra.

Brahma, depicted as an old man, mature and wise, is also said to be the source of knowledge. The theatrical arts, music, dance and stagecraft are said to be his gifts to the world.

Vishnu

The Preserver

नील सरोरुह स्याम तरुन अरुन बारिज नयन ।
करउ सो मम उर धाम सदा छीरसागर सयन ॥
मत्स्य : कूर्मो वराहश्च नरसिंहोदथ वामन
रामो रामश्च बुध्द : कल्की च ते दश ॥

 There were no earth-shaking tremors, no beautiful maiden whom his eyes would follow, when Vishnu, the second of the Hindu Triad was first mentioned in the Puranic description of the process of creation. He lay reclining on the coil of Seshnag, the king of serpents, on the still, tranquil, primeval waters of the ocean.

Vishnu's advent was peaceful; his world was complete, the picture of domestic bliss, with his consort Lakshmi – the Goddess of Fortune – by his side. He seemed to symbolise continuity and stability. From his navel rose a large lotus flower carrying Brahma – the Creator.

Having created the universe, Brahma realised the necessity for preservation, from the thousands of *asuras* or demons who were also born as a result of the process of creation. The universe was destined now to have a balance of power, as it were, between the forces of good and evil. Preservation meant action. So, from his own essence Brahma created a corporeal being – Vishnu, the spirit of action.

The name Vishnu is derived from the Sanskrit root *vis,* to pervade, and Vishnu is said to infuse his essence into all created things. Though Vishnu is generally considered the second deity of the Hindu Trinity, his followers, the Vaishnavas, consider him to be the most influential member of the Triad and believe that it was Vishnu who took on three aspects and creates, preserves and destroys.

Vishnu is different from the other two gods of the Trinity since in his

compassion he discards his celestial being and descends
into the world of mortals in his various incarnations to
deliver earth in times of danger. Vishnu descended to the
earth from his abode in Vaikunth, the archetypal picture of heaven,
with streets lined with gold and precious stones. Since Lakshmi, his
consort, is the Goddess of Wealth, she gives of her bounty generously.
Amidst all thissplendour, on white lotus blooms, sit Vishnu and Lakshmi,
as dazzling as the light of the sun.

He embodies the Vaishnava ideals of Hinduism. He lives in the
world, experiencing all the joys and sorrows of a householder, and
does not abandon the world as does Shiva – the Destroyer. He is seen
as loving and compassionate and each devotee worships him as his
own personal deity, following the cult of *bhakti* or devotion to a personal
god, where the love of the devotee is unselfish and adoring.

Vishnu, who holds sway over intervening time, and oversees stability
and continuity, is one of the gods of the Trinity in modern popular
Hinduism. In the *Vedas* however, he does not appear to be prominent,
and is referred to only as one among several gods. Yet he is mentioned
in all four *Vedas*. Sometimes he is said to be different forms of light,
and sometimes different positions of the sun. But the *Vedas* do hint
towards his future dominance.

In the *Satapatha Brahmana* (a part of the *Vedas*), it is said that the
gods became envious of Vishnu's rise to prominence, and cut off his
head. But to their alarm they realised that they could not do without
him, and begged the Ashwinis, the celestial physicians, to bring him
back to life, which the Ashwinis did.

In the *Bhagvata Purana* there is another story depicting the
superiority of Vishnu. The sages were performing a sacrifice on the
banks of the river Saraswati, when an argument erupted as to who
was the greatest – Brahma, Vishnu or Shiva. Bhrigu was sent to meet
all three and resolve this issue. Bhrigu approached the
abode of Brahma and to test him, walked in without
his permission. Brahma took this as an insult

but because Bhrigu was his son, he contained his anger. Bhrigu then proceeded to Mount Kailash to meet Shiva.

As Shiva came forward to embrace him, Bhrigu deliberately turned away and Shiva enraged at this affront, tried to smite him with his trident, but was pacified by his wife, Parvati.

Having assessed the two gods, Bhrigu went to Visnnu as he lay with his head on Lakshmi's lap. Vishnu, the perfect host, arose and welcomed him, apologising for the hurt his foot may have received from Vishnu's body. Bhrigu was so taken aback by his reception that he was unable to reply and tears gushed out from his eyes. When he recounted his experiences with the three gods to the sages, they were unanimous in their selection of Vishnu as the greatest, since he was free from impatience and passion.

Worship of Vishnu is supposed to mellow the emotions for he himself is the embodiment of mercy, benevolence and goodness.

The *Vishnu Purana* relates how Yama – the God of Death – cautioned his helpers not to touch those who were worshippers of Vishnu, saying, "Who through knowledge diligently adores the lotus foot of Hari (Vishnu), is released from all bonds of sin, and you must avoid him as fire fed with oil." Vishnu is known to be pleased with those who do good to others and those who are always desirous of the welfare of all creatures.

Vishnu is depicted as a tall, dark and handsome man with four arms. In one hand he holds a mace which is the power of knowledge, in another a conch shell, the symbol of the origin of existence, since it is from the waters, and when blown, has the primeval sound from which all creation began. The third hand holds the Sudarshan Chakra, the discus symbolic of the Universal Mind which can destroy all forms of ignorance and the demons of error. The lotus held in the fourth is the unfolding universe and also the notion of purity, since it retains its beauty in spite of its murky surroundings. On Vishnu's chest is the Kaustabha, a brilliant gem representing the consciousness manifested in all that shines, the sun, the moon and fire. On its left is a lock of hair named the Srivatsa

(the Beloved of Fortune), which is a mark of fortune.

Vishnu's emblems have become a cult by themselves. It is believed that the Shankha (conch shell), and Chakra, taking on a life of their own, are sent to earth to destroy evil. They are also worshipped as manifestations of Vishnu and in some temples appear without the anthropomorphic image. The image of Vishnu is depicted in three forms, either standing or the *sthanaka murthi*, the *asana murthi* or sitting posture and the *sayana murthi* or reclining form. Vishnu temples in south India sometimes have storeys in the central shrine, each storey being occupied by one image, beginning with the standing image at the ground floor.

One of the most fascinating attributes of Vishnu is that his worshippers can worship him in any form – *Yoga* for those who wish to meditate, *Bhoga* for those who want enjoyment, *Vira* for physical prowess and *Abhicharaka*, especially for kings and rulers who wish to conquer their enemies. The importance of each form is established by the number of deities surrounding him. There could be Bhudevi (the Earth Goddess), his consort Lakshmi, the snake Seshnag, and his vehicle Garuda, part human and part bird, and a host of other celestial beings. It is significant to note that the four *dhams*, or Hindu pilgrimages said to be gateways to heaven, are dedicated to Vishnu or his *avatars*.

The Bhagavata Puran says that "the favour of Vishnu is to be attained by pure, unselfish love and not by high birth, vast learning, boundless wealth or worldly things".

Garuda

King Garuda, best beyond compare
Of birds who wing the fields of air.

~ *Ramayana*

Half-man, half-eagle, Garuda is the vehicle of Vishnu and is mentioned in several stories connected with him. It is said that he is the son of the sage Kashyapa and Vinti, the daughter of Daksha, who is also known as the father of Parvati. According to the *Vishnu Purana*, she is said to have laid an egg, out of which, after 500 years, appeared the bird-like form of Garuda. Soon after his birth, his mother was held captive by his step-mother Kadru, the mother of the Nagas or snakes. Her release could only be effected by giving the Nagas the nectar of the gods, *amrit*, which was guarded by Indra and his followers. Garuda stole the nectar from Indra to procure her release, telling Indra that he could steal it back from the Nagas once his mother had been released. The pot of nectar was laid on a stack of *kusa* grass, but before the Nagas could taste it, Indra dextrously snatched it away. The Nagas then licked off the drops from the sharp-edged grass, thus lacerating their tongues which have remained forked ever since.

It was while he was returning with the pot of nectar that he met Vishnu and became his carrier or *vahana*.

Garuda is depicted as half-man, with the body and head of a man, but with bird's wings and a prominent beak. Being the arch enemy of serpents because of their treatment of his mother, he is sometimes shown with a snake in his beak, and is often surrounded by snakes. He is sometimes shown as having four arms, one carrying an umbrella, another the pot of nectar, while the other hands are in the attitude of adoration. When he carries Vishnu, two hands support him, while the other two are in attitudes of supplication.

Garuda was said to have helped Rama too in the *Ramayana*. Rama and Lakshmana were wounded by an army of snakes sent by Indrajit, Ravana's son; and it was Garuda, the enemy of all serpents, who came to their aid and enabled them to carry on the war.

He sometimes has the head and wings of a bird, and a human body; in other representations he has the body of a bird surmounted by a human head and the claws of a bird.

The Ten Avatars

Whenever the demons and the wicked troubled the gods and the good,

O Lord, you incarnated yourself to end their distress

~ Vishnu Chalisa

With the curse of Shukra and Bhrigu, Vishnu was condemned to be born on earth several times. Thus, whenever lawlessness or evil reared its head, Vishnu left Vaikunth and descended to earth to restore righteousness and to destroy evil. There are several *avatars* (incarnations), of which the most commonly accepted are the *dashavatars* or the 10 incarnations. The first three, which are not so popular today, the Matsya (fish), Kurma (tortoise), and Varaha (boar), deal with the myths of creation and are animal reincarnations. The *avatars* depict the process of evolution, going from the lower forms of life (the first three) to the part-animal part-human Narasimha, and gradually culminate in the heroic and human *avatars* of Rama and Krishna. The last two, Buddha and Kalki (yet to come), are the saviours who assist mortals to attain *nirvana* or salvation.

Matsya *The Fish*

As Brahma slept at the end of his creation of one age, the Age of Truth(Satya Yuga), the demon Hayagriva stole the words of the *Vedas* which came from his lips. Soon the demons were causing devastation, and the time was right for Vishnu to come to earth as the fish (Matsya). One day, when Manu, the first man, was offering water as an oblation to Surya, a tiny fish appeared in his hand. It pleaded with him to save its life from the larger fish in the river. Manu put it in an earthen pot full of water, but it soon outgrew the pot. After that he deposited the fish first in the smaller tributaries, then in the river Ganga, both of which could not long contain the fish. Awed by this transformation, as he was putting the fish in the ocean, it smiled at him and revealed its divine nature. It then warned Manu of an impending deluge and advised him to build a large boat and board it with seven rishis or wise men, one of each kind of animal and the seeds of each plant. Manu did as he was told and events followed according to the prediction of the fish. As the boat rose with the water, the fish appeared and fastened itself to the boat by means of the serpent Vasuki and led it safely to the top of the mountains. As the floods receded, Manu descended to the plains with all the occupants of the boat and started procreation for the next *yuga*.

In its images, Matsya is easily identified with Vishnu because it carries the emblems of Vishnu, the conch and the discus, and is sometimes accompanied by Lakshmi and Bhudevi. It is depicted as white in colour, either as a fish or as half-man half-fish.

Kurma *The Tortoise*

The story of this incarnation is associated with the churning of the ocean to obtain from it the *amrit* or nectar to give the gods the strength to fight the *asuras*. The sage Durvasa had cursed Indra to lose his sovereignty over the three worlds, because he imagined Indra had spurned the gift of a garland given to him by Durvasa. As the *asuras* periodically defeated the gods, Indra appealed to Vishnu, who advised the gods to churn the ocean of milk to obtain the nectar that would give them strength. He told them to immerse all the medicinal herbs in it and use Mount Mandhara as a churning stick. The gods were advised to take the help of the *asuras* to uproot the mountain and to promise them an equal share of the ambrosia. When the gods protested, Vishnu said he would take care of the consequences. The snake was used as a rope for the churning stick – the mountain. The *asuras*, suspecting foul play, chose to stay close to the serpent's head, while the gods were at the tail end. As foreseen by Vishnu, the *asuras* became weak from the hot and poisonous breath of the snake, while the gods were cooled by the breeze.

With the vigorous pulling, the mountain sank to the bottom of the ocean and it was then that Vishnu took the form of a tortoise to support the mountain on his back. As the churning continued, 14 precious articles emerged from it. Vishnu claimed four of them – the conch shell, the bow, the mace and the jewel Kaustabha. Lakshmi, his consort, was also one of the gifts of the ocean. At last came Dhanwantri – the Lord of Physicians – carrying the bowl of *amrit* – the drink of immortality. The *asuras* were the first to reach the bowl and snatch it from Dhanwantri's hand. But true to form, they quarelled over who should drink it first. Vishnu, taking the form of a beautiful woman, Mohini, took the pot from them and asked the gods and the demons to sit in two rows while she distributed the nectar to them. But as soon as all the gods had been served, Mohini disappeared with the bowl.

The Kurma *avatar* sometimes has the body of a human with the head of a tortoise or vice versa. He is either black or golden in colour, and his parted lips suggest the recitation of the *Vedas*. He also carries the Shankh and Chakra and like Vishnu, two of his hands are held in the blessing (*varada*) or protection (*abhaya*) poses.

VARAHA *The Boar*

The demon Hiranyaksha, having obtained a boon from Brahma, after years of austerities, that no man, god or beast could kill him, somehow omitted to include the boar species. He then went on a voyage of destruction and persecution, finally throwing the earth into the depths of the sea, and stealing the *Vedas* from Brahma. When men and gods could take it no longer, they appealed to Vishnu, and he assumed the *avatar* of a boar, killed Hiranakshya, and restored the earth to its original place. Vishnu is then said to have divided the earth into seven continents and beautified it with valleys and mountains.

The Varaha *avatar* was gigantic in size and black in colour with fearful white teeth and flashing eyes. He is usually depicted with his face to the ground, sniffing the earth or carrying it in his arms.

NARASIMHA *The Man-Lion*

This is one of the more popular stories of the *Puranas* and is still told on special occasions, particularly during the spring festival of Holi, since one of the myths connected with this colourful celebration tells the story of Prahlad and his aunt Holika, a sister of Raja Hiranyakashyapa. Hiranyaksha and Hiranyakashyapa were brothers who had been cursed by Vishnu to be born as *asuras*. Hiranyaksha appears in the story of the Varaha *avatar*.

But like the *asuras* in many other stories, they too had been granted a boon by Brahma, that they would be invulnerable to gods, men and beasts. Hiranyakashyapa had some additional conditions granted to him. He could not be killed by day or by night; neither inside nor outside the house; nor by gods, men or animals.

His arrogance made him so bold as to compare himself with the Supreme Being. He forbade the mention or worship of God in his kingdom, but much to his chagrin his own son Prahlad was a great devotee of Vishnu, and refused to obey his father's dictates.

Hiranyakashyapa's efforts to make him give up his belief only strengthened Prahlad's faith. And Vishnu too assisted him through the tortures inflicted on him by his father, who tried various means such as drowning, imprisoning him in a cell full of poisonous snakes or casting him down from a high mountain, but with Vishnu's blessings, he remained unhurt. Hiranyakashyapa tried destroying Prahlad by fire, by making him sit in his aunt Holika's lap on a pyre. Holika had been granted a boon that no fire could ever consume her. But with Vishnu on his side, Prahlad came out unscathed while Holika perished in the fire. To this day, on the occasion of Holi, fires are lit and Holika is burnt symbolically. Hiranyakashyapa was at his wits' end and taunted Prahlad about the omnipresence of Vishnu, asking him how he could prove that God was present among them. So saying, he struck a pillar with his foot and to his astonishment, a strange figure, the half-man half-lion Narasimha, came out in his awesome splendour, put Hiranyakashyapa on his lap and tore out his entrails with his claws, while sitting on the doorstep.

To circumvent Brahma's boon, Narasimha was neither man nor beast, the event took place at twilight which was neither day nor night, and he was killed neither inside nor outside the house since it was on the doorstep.

Narasimha still has an independent cult known throughout Orissa and the eastern coast. The events of this story are believed to have taken place in the temple town of Ahobilam in Andhra Pradesh, where a festival is still celebrated commemorating the apparition of Narasimha.

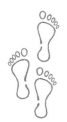

VAMANA *The Dwarf*

Bali, the king of the demons, became so powerful that he usurped the three *lokas* or worlds of Indra. Indra, exiled from his heaven, prayed to Vishnu to come to his aid or the *asuras* would overrun the universe. So Vishnu was born as Vamana, a child of Aditi, who was also Indra's mother. Vamana went to Bali's court as an ascetic begging for alms, and even though he was warned that this was Vishnu reincarnated, Bali agreed to give him whatever he wished for. Vamana asked for that portion of the earth that he could cover in three strides. Bali, little realising his folly, generously granted him his wish.

Vamana measured the earth with one of his strides, then he increased in size to such an extent that in two strides he measured the three *lokas* and finding no space for the third stride, he put his foot on Bali's head and pushed him into the underworld, relieving the earth of evil, while the gods and men were grateful to him for having saved the world.

The Vamana *avatar* is depicted with one arm outstretched begging for the earth and one foot raised to begin his conquest. Vishnu's three strides represent the rising, the culmination and the setting of the sun.

PARASURAMA *Rama with the Axe*

Vishnu was born as Parasurama to contain the might of the Kshatriyas, who were becoming more powerful than the Brahmins. He was born as the son of the hermit Jamdagni and his wife Renuka. Parasurama literally means 'Rama with the Axe', and this axe was given to him by Shiva, for the defence of the Brahmins.

Kartavirya, a Kshatriya king, once visited Jamdagni's hermitage and even though his wife Renuka honoured them as guests, Kartavirya took advantage of her hospitality and stole Kamadhenu, the cow of plenty. When Jamadagni discovered the loss of his cow, he followed the king, overpowered and killed him, and brought back the cow. When the king's son heard this, he in turn killed Jamadagni, thus incurring the wrath of Parasurama, who swore to kill all Kshatriyas in revenge for his father's death.

He is supposed to have destroyed them all in 21 battles and it is the common belief that the present-day Kshatriyas are the children of Brahmin fathers by Ksahtriyas mothers, since Parasurama destroyed the last male.

The figure of Parasurama is strong and imposing carying the axe or *parasu* in his right hand. His hair is matted and his body adorned with jewels.

RAMA *The Righteous King*

This is a story again of the arrogance of the demons and the gods' way of dealing with it through an *avatar*. Ravana, the king of Lanka, wallowing in the belief that Brahma and Shiva's boon in return for his austerities would grant him invulnerability, spent his time in killing and destruction. Brahma and Shiva looked on helplessly and asked men to turn to Vishnu for help. Vishnu, agreed to descend as a human in the *avatar* of Rama.

So Rama's reincarnation was specifically for the destruction of Ravana. And with him were incarnated several other deities, including Hanuman.

Rama was born to Kaushalya, one of the three queens of Raja Dashrath, king of Ayodhya. About the same time, Vishnu's consort Lakshmi, was born as Sita, the daughter of Dharti or Mother Earth, though she was brought up by King Janaka, who had found her abandoned in the fields .

Dashrath had performed a *yagna* (sacrifice) for the birth of sons and the gods bestowed on him four sons – Rama, the son of Kaushalya; Bharata, the son of Kaikeyi; and Lakshmana and Shatrughana, born of Sumitra.

Rama showed great promise of military strength even as a young child and both Rama and Lakshmana were trained under the guidance of the *guru* Vishwamitra.

In the adjoining kingdom lived Janaka, who had brought up the young princess Sita, as his own daughter. Wishing to find the perfect husband for Sita, he announced a *swayamvara*, a bethrothal ceremony in which

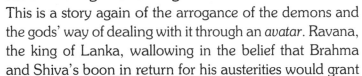

the girl garlands the man of her choice from amongst the many invited by her father.

There was a competition whereby Shiva's mighty bow and arrow had to be handled by the many suitors who wished for Sita's hand in marriage. Rama not only picked up the mighty bow but even broke it into two, and thereby won Sita as his bride.

But their happiness was short-lived because of the envy of Rama's step-mother Kaikeyi. Kaikeyi wanted her son Bharata to be king, but since Rama, being the eldest was the natural heir, she reminded Dashrath about the two boons he had promised her as return for having once saved his life. She now demanded that her son be installed as king and Rama sent off to a 14-year exile in the forest. Dashrath, living by the rules of *dharma*, could not go back on his word, and hence, sorrowfully acquiesced to her.

Rama, always the good son, did not want to bring dishonour to his father and left Ayodhya along with Lakshmana, his brother and Sita, who insisted on accompanying him. The exile of his son caused Dashrath to die of grief . Bharata, angry with his mother's cruel demand, followed Rama to the forest, entreating him to return and ascend the throne. But Rama refused to go back on his word to his dead father, so Bharata took his wooden sandals and symbolically placed them on the throne, awaiting his return.

Rama's exile accelerated the events for which Vishnu had actually come down to earth in this *avatar*– the destruction of the demon Ravana.

It all started with Shurpanakha, Ravana's sister, who having seen Rama in the forest, fell in love with him. Since Rama rejected her, she went to Lakshmana, who in anger cut off her nose, symbolic of loss of honour and respect. To avenge this insult, Shurpanakha persuaded her brother Ravana to kill Rama and artfully aroused his interest by praising Sita's beauty, saying that he could have her if Rama was no more. Ravana asked his magician uncle Maricha, to take the form of a golden deer to arouse Sita's interest.

Sita, seeing this golden deer, insisted that

Rama bring it to her. Lakshmana too was persuaded to follow Rama and when both the brothers were out, Ravana abducted Sita, keeping her a prisoner in the Ashoka Vatika (a garden full of ashoka trees) since he was afraid to bring her into his house against her wishes, fearing the curse of his nephew Nala-Kubera, who had pronounced that his uncle would perish if he ever took a woman against her wishes. So Ravana waited, confident that Sita would eventually fall for his charms, not realising that the abduction itself had set the curse in motion.

Rama and Lakshmana gathered a force of monkeys, bears and other forest inhabitants, led by the devoted Hanuman, and attacked Lanka. After several battles, Ravana and his evil brothers were killed and Sita rescued. There was great rejoicing in the land and to this day the victory of Rama over Ravana is celebrated as Dassera. After prayers and offerings to Rama and Sita, there is the symbolic killing of Ravana in each household.

Most north Indian cities have what is known as the Ram Lila ground, where the public burning of the effigies of Ravana and his brothers takes place.

Then comes the festival of Diwali, the triumphant return of Rama to Ayodhaya after his exile. The city of Ayodhya was aglow with oil lamps, a symbol of auspiciousness, a tradition carried on for centuries, as Hindus celebrate Diwali today.

Inspite of the jubilation surrounding the return of the exiled king, there was one dark cloud hovering over the lives of Rama and Sita – the secret whisperings and misgivings among the people of Ayodhya about Sita's chastity, while living as Ravana's prisoner. Rama, now in his position as the ideal king, could not allow any doubts about his consort and Sita had to go through an ordeal by fire which exonerated her, but the humiliation and suffering made her give up the court and worldly life and retire to the forest *ashram* of Valmiki, the future author of the *Ramayana*, where she gave birth to twins, Luv and Kush.

As the twins grew up, they were discovered by Rama, who entreated that Sita and his sons should return to Ayodhya. But Sita's time on earth was drawing to a close and she is said to have been swallowed up by her mother, Dharti (the earth). Soon after, Rama too decided that the life of this *avatar* was over and he gave up his mortal body and ascended to his abode, Vaikunth, as Vishnu.

The image of Rama is usually shown with both Sita and Lakshmana on either side. He is dark in colour and dressed in yellow, with a crown on his head. He has only two arms as a human incarnation, one hand holding the *dhanush* (bow) and the other holding the *baan* (arrow) as most of his earthly life was spent fighting the armies of Ravana. In most representations, his devoted Hanuman kneels at his feet with folded palms.

Devotion to Rama is an important part of Hindu belief. The greeting 'Rama-Rama', the concept of *Ram-Rajya*, the ideal kingdom, reveal that Rama is a symbol in the Hindu social, religious and political ethos. Sita is always held up as the ideal wife, sharing her husband's misfortunes with grace. Yet, she finally asserted herself by leaving him when he repeatedly put the opinion of his subjects above his own conviction of her fidelity.

Rama was perhaps a historical figure – one of the Aryan chieftains who defeated the original inhabitants represented by Ravana. But over the years he has been accepted as a reincarnation of Vishnu, and is seen as the preserver of good over evil.

Rama is seen as the ideal, archetypal king, as also the embodiment of family and filial values. He was the ideal son, then the ideal husband during his exile, the concerned brother, earning his siblings' love and respect and then the ideal king when he does ascend the throne, putting his duty as king even above his own beloved wife and sons. He is the true follower of the Hindu *dharma* which enjoins doing the right action in the right context, without thought of reward or punishment.

The story of Rama's historic deeds and flawless character is told best by Tulsidas, the saint poet who wrote *Ramcharitmanas* in such simple language, that it caught the minds of the masses and is responsible for the stories being passed on orally even in the remotest parts of India.

The legend of Rama is still a living tradition even in some countries of South-East Asia, particularly Sri Lanka, Indonesia and Cambodia, where there are temples to Rama and performances of the *Ramayana* are common occurrences.

KRISHNA

Surrender then thy actions unto Me, live in Me ,
concentrate thine intellect on Me and think always of Me.

~ Krishna in the *Gita*

In the city of Mathura, a child was born in prison to Devaki and Vasudeva. The elements announced his birth as it was the month of Shravan, when rains lash the country and lightning and thunder keep most people indoors. So it was fortunate that the prison guards slept under a spell and the prison gates opened miraculously by themselves as Vasudeva carried his infant son, surreptitiously hidden in a basket on his head, to the safety of Gokul. The river goddess Jamuna parted her waters to allow Vasudeva to cross with his precious burden and deposit the infant with his foster parents, Nanda and Yashoda.

The infant was no other than Krishna, who later became one of the most popular deities of the Hindus.

In the *Mahabharata*, Krishna claims that he is "a portion of the portion" of the essence of Vishnu, but this eighth incarnation superseded the worship of Vishnu and all his *avatars* so that by the present century, Vishnu has faded into the background and the cult of Krishna is almost synonymous with Hinduism.

The child Krishna is mentioned only at the

end of the 5th century or the early 6th century AD. It is said that due to the rapacious tendencies of the evil forces, specially of Kansa, the Earth appealed to Indra to rid the world of this tyranny, failing which she herself would descend to *pataal* or the nether regions. Indra went to Brahma, who guided him to Shiva, who in his turn suggested that Vishnu be approached since he was by now well-versed in assuming the human form. Vishnu plucked two strands of hair from his head, one black and the other white. The white hair was the embryo out of which his earth-born brother, Balarama, was born to Rohini, one of the wives of Kansa's brother-in-law, Vasudeva. The other black hair became the wife of Vasuudeva – Devaki, Kansa's sister, and the mother of Krishna. This is cited as the reason for the dark colour of this deity.

Kansa, who had usurped the throne of his old father Ugrasena, had been warned by a prophecy that he would be killed by one of Devaki's children. Fearing for his life, Kansa had Devaki and her husband Vasudeva put into prison and to protect himself, killed six of their children. The seventh child was Nidra, an incarnation of the Devi, who ascended to heaven as soon as she was snatched from her mother's arms by Kansa and derided him saying that the one who was his slayer was still alive in Gokul.

Kansa ordered every newborn male child in Gokul to be slain, but Krishna escaped all these attempts. Kansa's sister Putana, was sent to feed the baby at her poisoned breast, but when the villagers found them, they saw that it was Putana who lay dead, while Krishna played happily in her lap.

In this constant struggle between good and evil, the people of Gokul and adjoining Vrindavan, witnessed the supernatural powers of the boy Krishna and realised that he was no ordinary mortal. They saw how the child had the strength to uproot two strong arjuna trees when he was tied to them as a punishment, thus liberating the two sons of Kubera (the God of Wealth), who had dwelt in them because of a curse. His companions were astonished when Krishna entered the river Jamuna to challenge the serpent Kalia, who was contaminating the waters and destroying the foliage on the banks of the river. They waited with bated breath for the outcome which spelt sure death for the child Krishna. Instead, they saw the many-headed Kalia emerge from the still waters with Krishna dancing on his hood, while the female serpents paid obeisance.

Complete faith in his godhead came when even Indra, the feared God of the Sky, whose anger could spell flood and destruction in their daily lives, acknowledged the superiority of Krishna. Indra created rain and storm in the region surrounding Gokul and Mathura, to punish his devotees who were so enamoured of Krishna that they seemed to have forgotten Indra. Krishna lifted the mountain Govardhan on his little finger and gathered all the living creatures under it to save them from the deluge. Ever since then, the mountain Govardhan has also been worshipped, and devotees make offerings and perform *parikrama* (ritual circumambulations) around the sacred mountain.

Yashoda, Krishna's foster-mother had already had premonitions of the divinity of Krishna and she was convinced when one day, suspecting him of having swallowed some mud, she asked him to open his mouth. When the child Krishna complied with her demand , she was amazed to see the whole world in his mouth. She embraced him in wonder, and considered herself blessed to have fostered an incarnation of divinity.

From childhood to boyhood and manhood, the worship of Krishna encompasses every phase of his life. He is Balagopal, the infant Krishna crawling on all fours with a *laddoo* (round shaped sweet) in his hand. He has a crown of peacock feathers on his head, and is the delight of all the mothers in the villages of Gokul, who cannot fathom the mysteries of this beautiful baby who has killed Putana, and overturned a wagon as he lay in its shade, to draw attention to his hunger.

The worship of the infant Krishna is widespread and the image of Balagopal or Laddoogopal as he is affectionately known, is specially brought out in all temples during Janamashtmi, the birth of Krishna, which falls in August. He is placed in a cradle and offerings of milk and curd are made to him in this stage of infancy. The *puja* at midnight, the time he was said to have been born, at the Dwarkadheesh temple in Mathura, is so well known that the temple proceedings are even broadcast on radio and shown on television.

The young Krishna, dallying with the *gopis* or milkmaids in the forests of Vrindavan, has been recaptured in miniature paintings, classical music, and dance. This depiction has been seen as erotic or with sexual undertones perhaps because it is this aspect which has been magnified by art. But in the songs of the saint poets of medieval India, it is interpreted as the intense devotion of the devotee pining for a union with God, and the image of two lovers being drawn to each other was the simplest way of explaining it to a vast mass of people. The story of the *Raas Lila*, seen in innumerable paintings in which several Krishnas are seen dancing with the milkmaids, symbolises the love and concern of God for each individual. Since each of the *gopis* longs to dance with him, Krishna multiplies his form to partner each of them, emphasizing the personal relationship of the devotee with God.

Krishna is seen later as the King of Dwarka, a city on the extreme west coast of India, which is one of the four *dhams* or pilgrimages. He is the embodiment of truth and justice, the ideal king, like Rama in the *Ramayana*. His wife is the beautiful Rukmini, sister of Rukmin, the king of Vidharba, and friend of Krishna's enemy, Kansa. When Rukmini married Krishna against her brother's wishes, Rukmin attacked Krishna's army but was routed by Krishna's brother, Balarama.

From king to philosopher-advisor in the great epic *Mahabharata*, Krishna's last phase is perhaps the most enduring since it is in this role as charioteer to Arjuna, the leader of the army of the Pandavas, that Krishna reveals himself as God.

Arjuna, unable to reconcile himself to the idea of going to battle with his cousins, the Kauravas, is encouraged by Krishna to take heart and perform his duty, which is to destroy the evil perpetuated by the Kauravas, irrespective of his relationship with them. Krishna talks at length about the value of *karma* (action), that is, the performance of one's duty with detachment, without thought of result or reward. Arjuna's agonised plea "My Lord ! How can I, when the battle rages, send an arrow through Bheeshma (Arjuna's beloved uncle who was on the side of the enemy) and Drona (his *guru* and mentor) who should receive my reverence ? "

And Krishna says that in order to fulfill one's social obligations one has to do one's appointed work and yet remain uninvolved in its consequences, "Just as the unwise act, being attached to their actions, even so should the wise act, O Bharata, but without attachment and only with a view to promoting the solidarity of society.

Dedicate thyself to Me, worship Me, sacrifice all for Me, prostrate thyself before Me, and to Me shalt thou surely come."

Having fulfilled all the tasks for which he had come down to earth as an *avatar*, Krishna realised that his end was near. According to a curse pronounced by the Rishi Durvasa, Krishna was to die of a wound on his foot. This came about because once when Durvasa had visited him, Krishna had overlooked the ritual of wiping his feet after his meal. Durvasa, known for his impatience and bad temper, had cursed Vishnu and the prophecy was to be fulfilled. Durvasa had also cursed the Yadavs of Dwarka, Krishna's clansmen, who, he said, would be destroyed by an iron club which would be born of Krishna's grandson Samba, because he had shown disrespect to the sage.

Krishna retreated to the countryside from where he had first come, and lay down under a tree. A hunter, Jara, mistaking him from a distance, for a deer, shot an arrow into his only vulnerable spot, his foot, and thus fulfilled the prophecy of Krishna's end and his liberation from his human form.

Krishna as a deity captured the imagination and devotion of the Hindus to such an extent, that he himself was seen in several forms, the most widely worshipped being Shrinathji in Nathdwara (the gate to God) in Rajasthan and Jagannath in Puri, in the eastern province of Orissa.

A religious preacher of the 16th century, Vallabha, while on a pilgrimage to Mathura, is said to have had a dream in which Krishna appeared to him and directed him to preach the *Pushti Marg*, the way to salvation by complete devotion and subservience to God.

It was here also that Vallabha discovered the icon of Shrinathji which was found in a hole in the mountain Govardhan, where Krishna had imprinted his image when he lifted the mountain up on his little finger. The image had been seen only partly for a long time, but on the day Vallabha was born, the whole image appeared out of the mountain. Shrinathji became the central point of the worship of what became known as the Vallabha Sampradaya, after its founder. When Aurangzeb, the fanatic Moghul ruler, attacked Mathura and ordered the destruction of temples, the image of Shrinathji was smuggled out of Govardhan and installed in Nathdwara, near Udaipur.

Vallabha preached that the image is not merely a symbolic form of the deity, but Krishna himself in another manifestation. The devotees of Shrinathji look upon him as a living god, and their worship centers around the re-enactment of all the scenes in Krishna's life, leading them to *moksha* or eternal bliss. Shrinathji is bathed, clothed, fed and offered presents and these ceremonies are watched by thousands of devotees who throng the temple.

Shrinathji is very dark in colour, suggesting a link with tribal gods, has elongated eyes and a broad nose. His left hand is raised up, symbolic of his holding Govardhan on it. His body is covered with jewellery and he has the peacock crown on his head.

The image of Lord Jagannath of Puri is supposed to be the work of the architect of the gods, Vishwakarma. It is said that the bones of Krishna were discovered in the forest and brought to King Indraduma of Orissa. The king requested Vishwakarma to make a wooden image of Krishna to house the relics.

Vishwakarma consented to do so, provided no one looked at the image before it was completed. The king agreed, but curiosity got the better of him and one day he visited Vishwakarma to see the progress of the image. Vishwakarma, angry at being disturbed, left the image half finished. Indraduma appealed to Brahma and he is said to have given the image eyes and a soul so that it could be worshipped. This image became famous throughout the country and is, like Dwarka, one of the four *dhams* or pilgrimages. But to this day, Jagannath has no arms or feet. He is always shown with his brother Balarama and sister, Subhadra.

Puri is the scene of one of the most famous *rath-yatras* or chariot festivals in India. Once a year, the image is carried in procession on a gigantic chariot pulled by thousands of devotees who consider this action one of the steps towards salvation.

The worship of Krishna was given an impetus with the advent of the *bhakti* cult which advocated belief in a personal God and a loving adoration of this God as a means of salvation. Krishna was child, lover, friend, king and teacher and symbolised the pursuit of happiness and bliss.

The *bhakti* tradition found expression through devotees who roamed the countryside singing hymns or *kirtans* to Krishna. It was these songs, composed in the vernacular, as opposed to the obscure Sanskrit verses of the older Hindu scriptures, that made the *bhakti* cult popular. They had an emotional appeal for the less educated strata of society and were soon picked up by people of all ages and backgrounds, fostering a unity hitherto unknown in the religion, riddled as it was by caste distinctions. Surdas, Mirabai, Kabir, Raskhan, all sang of the intense longing of the devotee for his God, a God for whom he gave up everything but who still remained elusive.

> *Don't go, don't*
> *Lifter of Mountains*
> *Let me offer a sacrifice — myself — beloved,*
> *to your beautiful face.*
>
> ~ Mirabai

THE BUDDHA

By His words as Buddha, Vishnu deludes the heretics.

~ Bhagavata Purana

It is difficult to reconcile the idea of Buddha as an *avatar* of Vishnu since the Buddhists as a cult were persecuted by the followers of the Brahminical religion. Perhaps the Brahmins seeing power slipping out of their hands because of the influence of Buddhism, wished to prove a common link between the two religions.

Thus Buddha was amalgamated as an *avatar* in a very clever way to subjugate the rival religion. Buddha was not the usual *avatar* of Vishnu , reincarnated to destroy evil; in fact, he was a negative influence, drawing the enemies of the gods to himself and thus weakening and destroying them, or making them turn back to the old faith and the established gods.

Buddha's teaching as an *avatar* differ greatly in interpretation from those adhered to by his followers. He preached that the world was not created by a Supreme Being and there is no God. The Hindu Trinity are just ordinary mortals. Caste distinctions and *dharma* (way of life) have no meaning and death was the end of existence since both heaven and earth were experienced on earth itself. Physical and sensual pleasures were advocated since the physical self must be indulged before it turned to dust. To preach this doctrine, even Lakshmi was reincarnated as a female monk of the Buddhist order.

The *Skanda Purana* tells the story of how Vishnu actually assumed this *avatar*. Because of the presence of evil on earth, the gods withheld rains for six successive years causing a dire famine. Brahma, moved by the prayers of the inhabitants of the earth, searched for a good king, and the only one he could find was Ripanjaya, who would be favourable to the gods so that they would replenish the earth. Ripanjaya agreed only on condition that none of the gods would interfere with him and that men would be beholden only to him for their happiness. Even Shiva was asked to vacate his home at Kashi. Brahma agreed, not wishing to disappoint his followers. So Ripanjaya, now renamed Devodasa, ruled for 8000 years, bringing prosperity to the people. But the gods, used to having their way, soon grew jealous as men on earth seemed to forget them. It was then that Vishnu was asked by Shiva and the other gods to wean people away from Devodasa's influence and he came down as Buddha, drawing people away from the good influence of Devodasa, till he, in despair, relinquished his throne in favour of his son and was taken by Shiva to Kailash.

Vishnu having effected the change on earth, abandoned his heretical teachings and returned to heaven.

It is interesting to note that though the other *avatars* are mythical, the Buddha *avatar* is historical. The Buddha *avatar* was probably included at a time when the influence of Buddhism was declining between the 10th-12th century and the Brahmins could safely allow an interaction between the two religions. It was also easier as both Vishnu and Buddha were benign and seen as saviours of mankind. The *avatar* bears a close resemblance to representations of Buddha, with a knot on top of his head, seated on a lotus seat in a position of meditation. The ears are long and pendant, and he is seen with one palm uplifted towards his disciples in a gesture of teaching.

KALKI

In the twilight of this age, when all kings will be thieves, the Lord of the Universe will be born as Kalki.

~ Bhagavata Purana

Most Hindus talk of the present age as *Kali Yuga* or the Dark Age, the Age of Strife. And many of the *Puranas* discuss this age when barbarians will become powerful, piety will decrease and social and spiritual life would have degenerated to its lowest level. Wealth and sensual pleasures will be sought after, rather than love and spiritual values, and driven by their avaricious rulers, the people will take refuge in forests and valleys and live on fruits and leaves.

Clothes will be replaced by the bark of trees and people will lead an animal existence at the mercy of the elements. In short, civilisation would have come full circle and life expectancy will not exceed 23 years. As men pray for deliverance, as they have done from time immemorial, *Vishnu* will come down in this avatar. He will be born in an eminent Brahmin family and will be endowed with super-human qualities.

He is depicted sometimes with the face of a horse with a man's body, red and very fierce looking. Sometimes he is described as a white man, and in Pahari (miniature paintings from the hill districts) paintings, as a dark warrior. But in all these representations, what is common is the blazing sword, since Kalki will be fighting evil with his sword, punishing evil-doers and then destroying the world, so that a new and golden age will be re-established, and once again the process of creation with Brahma as Creator will begin.

Shiva

The Destroyer

मुख्यो भगस्तु प्रकृतिर्भगवान शिव उच्यते ।
भगवान भोगदाता हि नान्यो भोगप्रदायका ॥

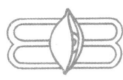 Sati, the daughter of Daksha, the god of established order, loved him; even as a child. Uma, the daughter of Himmavat, the king of the Himalayas, brought offerings of milk and water to his shrine; and Ravana offered his heads in sacrifice to him. This was Shiva, whose home was among the snows at Kailash.

In the *Mahabharata*, we have Arjuna and Krishna singing his praises, and yet the Gods mocked at him as a naked ascetic, a homeless wanderer and a being who haunted the unclean cemeteries and his father-in-law went so far as to forbid him to attend his *yagnas* (ritual sacrifices).

As Brahma appeared from the navel of Vishnu, two demons, Madhu and Kaitabha, attempted to kill him. Brahma, taken aback, prayed to Vishnu to protect him. Vishnu, pleased that Brahma, the Immense One, should beg him for a favour, expressed anger with the demons and from his frown emerged Shiva as Shambhu, wielding a trident, and destroying the demons.

Thus Shiva manifested himself as the Destroyer; and that attribute has stuck to him. Since all things are subject to decay and destruction, it was necessary to have the Destroyer, or indirectly the Re-creator; allowing all forms of existence to manifest themselves. Death is not death, but simply a manifestation into a new life. So he is Shiva, the Bright One.

His name does not appear in the *Vedas*, but he has been identified with Rudra, the Vedic god of storm. In one story from the *Vishnu Purana*, Brahma, desirous of having a son, wished for one and a little boy appeared sitting on his knee. But he would not stop weeping. When Brahma asked him the cause of his sorrow, he said that he had not been given a name. Brahma then named him Rudra – from *rud* which means 'to weep '.

Shiva was a difficult being to follow. He was a wanderer, sometimes living in the cold snows of the Himalayas, and sometimes descending to earth to reside in his favourite city of Kashi or Benaras. It was to this city that he repaired after having cut off Lord Brahma's head in a quarrel. Brahma, wishing to create again after a long sleep of a thousand years, created Ahankara or the consciousness of the ego.

But out of the darkness had already risen a form with three eyes, carrying a trident. An argument ensued, fuelled by Ahankara as to how each one came into being. Shiva, incensed at this question, cut off Brahma's head, but it would not fall out of his hand. Brahma, being the progenitor of all Brahmins, then created a giant to slay Shiva since he had committed the unforgivable sin of the murder of a Brahmin. To escape from him, Shiva came to Benaras and was absolved of his sin. Thus, Benaras became a city where one could absolve oneself of one's wrong actions. It was to do penance for this sin of brahminicide that Shiva was doomed to be a wandering ascetic.

Shiva's wife Parvati, once questions him about his austerities. When the heat of summer is unbearable, she asks why he does not have a roof to protect him from the vagaries of the seasons. "I am, O lovely one, without a shelter, a constant wanderer in forests", comes the reply. But his perceived poverty and asceticism does not make him subservient to any of the other gods. His meditative powers are phenomenal, building up his physical strength and giving him unlimited powers to perform miracles (and also to strengthen his image as a fertility god) and the strength thus acquired makes him superior to all the gods combined.

The *asuras* obtained a boon from Brahma so that they could become lords of three castles, from where they then constantly attacked the gods. The gods approached Brahma, who directed them to Shiva. Shiva agreed to transfer half his strength to them, but they found that they could not sustain it. In the end Shiva took half their strength and fired the arrow to destroy the demons, but decided not to return this extra strength to the gods, thus becoming the strongest god in the Universe.

So Shiva came to be known as Mahadeva or the Supreme Lord and his supreme creative power is worshipped as the *linga* or phallus. To explain this to the common man, the *Padma Purana* relates the story of the curse of the sage Bhrigu, who had wished to ascertain for himself who the greatest god from the Trinity was.When he went to visit Shiva, he was stopped at the door by a doorkeeper who informed him that no one could disturb Shiva and Parvati in their dalliance. Bhrigu, after having waited for some time, left after pronouncing the curse, that since Shiva preferred the embraces of Parvati to his meeting with Bhrigu, he would be doomed to be worshipped as the *linga* and *yoni*, instruments of desire and procreation.

The union suggested by the *linga* and the *yoni* is the link between the two worlds, one where life manifests itself, and the other where the spirit becomes incarnate; and the *linga* is the symbol of the Divine Creator, a symbol understood by even the most ignorant. The *linga* represents the joy of life and creation, as well as liberation after the control of desire. A mastery over the sexual instinct makes us dominate the physical as well the mental sphere. Shiva's vehicle, Nandi the bull, symbolises the instincts which often overrule the rational self; and Shiva, since he has conquered all desire, rides on the bull, signifying that only those who have acquired knowledge are masters of themselves. It was difficult to imagine Shiva the Destroyer; the Ascetic, the Wanderer, as the ideal husband for his daughter Sati, so Daksha, ignoring Sati's love for Shiva, invited all the gods except Shiva, for his daughter's *swayamvara*

(a gathering of princes, so that she could choose a husband by garlanding the one of her choice). Sati, disappointed at not finding Shiva, threw the garland into the air, praying to Shiva. Shiva manifested himself and took Sati away, much to Daksha's fury.

Daksha, as the god of established order and the Vedic ritual sacrifice, was a direct contradiction to Shiva, the *yogi* who believed in meditation and austerity and was available to all irrespective of their birth or status. Thus he was accused by Daksha and the other gods of being a teacher of the low born and hence not good enough to participate in the sacrifices of the *yagnas*.

This in effect was the struggle for supremacy between the Aryan and Vedic religions and the older religion of the Dravadian inhabitants of Bharat, which surprisingly still continues to this day, even after 2000 years.

So once again Daksha had a *yagna* and refused to invite his daughter Sati and her husband Shiva. Sati insisted on coming to the celebration at her father's house despite Shiva's protests. Daksha, finding her there, cursed her husband and belittled him before all the gods present. Sati, anguished by the insults heaped upon her absent husband, gave up her physical body by consigning herself to the flames, thus giving rise to the term *sati* – the one who burns herself on the funeral pyre. Shiva was in Kailash when heard the news, and was consumed by grief. He arrived at Daksha's house and let loose his hair, freeing the thousands of demons that resided there. These demons destroyed Daksha's sacrifice, and in battle, Shiva cut off his father-in-law's head, later repenting and giving Daksha a goat's head to bring him back to life. In the Puranic version, Shiva created an image of fire, Virabhadra, who destroyed the sacrifice and routed the gods.

Sati was born again as Uma, the daughter of Himmavat, the king of the Himalayas. In his grief, Shiva had given himself up to meditation on Mount Kailash, and refused to be tempted by any of the offerings and prayers of gods and mortals.

But the heavens and the earth were ravaged

by the evils of the demon Taraka who had been granted a boon by Brahma that he would be killed only by Shiva's son; Shiva, however, in his grief for Sati was not likely to produce a son. But they saw their salvation in Uma, who as she grew up, made her way to Kailash and also prayed and meditated hoping to arouse Shiva. The gods, delighted by this, sent Kama, the God of Love and his wife Rati, to interrupt Shiva's meditation so that the shaft of love would make him give in to Uma's entreaties. Shiva, in his anger at being disturbed by Kama, opened his third eye and reduced him to ashes. But the mischief had been done – he had looked upon Uma and fallen in love with her. So the couple retired to Kailash and out of this union was produced a seed which, nurtured by Uma's elder sister Ganga (the goddess of the river), became Kartikeya, the leader of the army of the gods, who killed Taraka.

So, though Shiva is Rudra the Fearsome, there is also the humane side to this god. He is impulsive and destroys but he is also repentant and gives back life as in the case of Daksha or Kama,who was restored to Rati in the spirit world. He is benevolent and bestows boons. He distributed the waters of the holy rivers to a parched earth. He is said to have caught the river Ganges in his locks to break her fall and prevent her from splitting the earth in two with her force. When the gods were churning the ocean to withdraw the *amrit* or nectar from it, suddenly the ocean threw up *kalakuta*, a poison slated to destroy all the creatures on earth.The gods, afraid, withdrew, all except Shiva, who gallantly drank the poison to save humanity. Parvati, alarmed for his life, leapt forward and held his throat, thus preventing the poison from being swallowed.The poison stuck in his throat, thus giving it a blue colour and a new name for him – Nilakanth, the Blue Throated.

Shiva's benevolent aspect is also depicted in his image as the Lord of Sleep, the remover of pain since sleep dilutes pain. He is the transcendent being, absorbing mortals who tire of life and action, pain and pleasure and enter into a peaceful state of non-existence. We fear death because we do not understand it; death means liberation from the bondage of life – like Shiva – destruction moving towards a new existence.

Shiva is depicted as a fair man covered with ashes; with four arms, five faces and three eyes on the face in front. His three eyes represent the three sources of light, the sun, the moon and fire and through these he can look into Time – past, present and future. The third is the inward-looking eye, destroying when it turns itself outwards. It is a powerful weapon, used for the destruction of his enemies. It is said that each *yuga* or period comes to an end when Shiva opens his third eye. The third eye was also opened to save the world. One day, Parvati playfully covered Shiva's eyes with her hand. Immediately the world was plunged into darkness and all life ebbed out of it. Suddenly, from Shiva's forehead, burst a flame which scorched the mountains, but dispelled the gloom.

Shiva's ornaments are skulls and snakes; the skull represents the revolution of Time and the appearance and disappearance of the human race. It also symbolises destruction at the end of a cycle, when all is destroyed except Shiva. The snakes represent death; and though Shiva is always surrounded by death, he himself is beyond its power. But the serpent also represents the dormant energy which is the source of all spiritual conquests and is said to be coiled at the base of the spinal cord.

The best known symbol of Shiva is the *trishul* or trident, representing the three aspects of nature, the *sattva*, *rajas* and *tamas*; the three functions, as Creator, Preserver and Destroyer; it also symbolises lightning, so Shiva is the god of storms. It also represents Shiva as the god of righteousness who has to punish wrong-doers. He holds a bow, Pinaka, made of a serpent with seven heads and poisonous teeth. This is used to help the gods in times of need. Shiva's battle-axe Parasu, was bequeathed to Parasurama, an incarnation of Vishnu, to destroy the warrior-race of the Kshatriyas, and his spear Pashupati, used for destruction at the end of each age, helped Arjuna in the battle of the *Mahabharata*.

Shiva's tiger skin depicts him as being beyond the power of nature, since the tiger, the vehicle of Shakti, is itself the symbol of that power. The skull is again used on the club, the *khatwanga*.

The *damru* or drum, becomes very important during Shiva's dance. He is Nataraja, the god of dance, said to have created 108 dances. some of them are gentle and slow, others are fearsome and rock the very foundations of the Universe. He is the god of rhythm, dancing for joy in anger or sorrow. Dance is the glory of Shiva, causing movement in the Universe. Not many are fortunate enough to have witnessed the spectacle of the *tandav*, the dance that destroys the world at the end of each cosmic cycle and then integrates it within the cosmic spirit, thus destroying *maya* or illusion. It is said that Seshnag, the serpent attendant of Lord Vishnu, saw this dance and was so dazzled by it that he forsook Vishnu for several years, hoping to catch a glimpse of it again. The gods assemble to watch it in wonder, the demons of the cemeteries are dazzled by it, thus bringing even evil spirits into the orbit of his spiritual power, hence he is known as Bhuteshwar, Lord of the Ghosts.

In one of his forms he is shown with five faces; he is the god of medicine and prayers for healing and recovery are made to him. In the absence of a temple, he is represented as a shapeless stone placed under a tree. He is said to possess people who suffer from epilepsy, and he is propitiated with offerings to be induced to leave the victim's body.

Shiva has been known as Swayambhu or the self-manifested, and is god of the five elements. His main temples are also dedicated to the elements – in Benaras, there is the water *linga*, in Kanchi (Conjeevaram), the earth *linga*, Chidambaram the ether *linga*, Kalahasti the air *linga* and the fire *linga* in Tiruvannamali.

Devi

The Mother Goddess

सर्वे वै देवा देवीमुपतस्थु : कासी त्वं महादेवी साब्रवीदहं
ब्रह्म-रूपिणी ।
मत्त: प्रकृतिपुरुषात्मकं जगत ।

She is the form of all that is conscious. The origin, the knowledge, the perception of reality, the instigator of intellect.

~ Devi Bhagvata Purana

 She is the *Shakti* or energy of the Universe, the power of the cosmic world which envelops the three *lokas* (worlds). The powerful god Shiva sings her praises and she pervades the thoughts of Brahma and Vishnu. She is said to be the creative aspect of Divinity, the power through which creation commences. She is the active female principle Prakriti, in union with the soul of the Universe, Purusa, manifested as one of the forms of the consort of Shiva – Parvati, Sati, Uma, Kali, Durga, Chandi, Gauri, Annapoorna.

Even Shiva, the ever-protective spouse, was breathless with fear when Sati revealed her several forms. She wished to return to her father's house, but Shiva, fearing for her, forbade her to go. Sati declared that she was the Mother of Creation and even Shiva had no right over her, and to Shiva's bewilderment he saw her first as Kanya, the gentle one; Shitala, the goddess of disease; Gauri, the earth mother; the fearsome Kali and Durga, the killer of demons, and he realised her strength and bowed to her wishes.

Shiva himself proclaims that without Shakti he is unable to create or destroy and that he is himself inert like a corpse.

Shakti is the all-powerful concept of the Mother Goddess, Devi, and her worship forms a very important part of Indian history and civilization.

All ancient civilizations had the mother goddess as an all-powerful concept. In India the worship of the Mother Goddess is seen first in the 5th – 6th century BC in images recovered from Mehrangarh, now in Baluchistan, even prior to the Indus Valley Civilisation. These figures were hand-modelled, mostly in clay and were obviously installed in all households to ward off evil and ill-health. The life-giving Mother image has always been associated with good luck and prosperity, and since survival depended on the bounties of Nature and the elements, the Earth was conceived as the Mother – *Dharti Mata* (Mother Earth).

The earth became her body and the mountains, revers and valleys represented her physical features. Vegetation was her adornment and when angry with her children, the Mother with held her bounty by drying up rivers and causing famine in the land. To circumvent her fickle nature, she had to be humoured and propitiated and thus all her aspects were to be worshipped.

Within the vast bosom of *Dharti Mata* were created her other incarnations, the river goddesses Ganga, Jamuna, Saraswati, all receiving their energy from the Supreme Goddess Mahadevi, who encompasses all the regional *devis*, including the ones in the broader Hindu pantheon. Thus Parvati was the child of the Mountains, Sita the child of the Earth and Lakshmi the daughter of the Ocean.

Fertility and life were associated with the Mother, so all forces of creation and the agricultural deities had naturally to be accepted as female. Since grain gathering, an important activity of the primarily agricultural Dravidians, was essentially a female domain, the female deities flourished. And the Mother was specially benevolent towards women, listening to their prayers and entreaties for the welfare of their husbands and children. The concept of the Divine Spirit as Mother was basic and could be comprehended by the simplest of minds. Human beings could please her with simple offerings and prayers. She could be invoked for specific afflictions such as disease or barrenness. One could pray to her for marriage or a good husband, and fast on specific days for the longevity and good health of one's spouse.

The coming of the Aryans, with their emphasis on vigour and masculinity, brought with it the Brahminical religion. Indra, Agni, Brahma, Vishnu, Shiva, were the gods who guided the destinies of the world. They were the archetypal Aryans, the role models for the conquering race. And yet, try as they might, the preachers of the new religion could not relegate the primordial beliefs in the Mother Goddess to the background. Not wishing to forego their influence on a large part of the population, they decided that wisdom lay in inculcating the Devi cult into the folds of the Brahminical beliefs. They saw the advantage of a 'marriage' between the gods and the ever-powerful Devi, thus effectively subjugating the female to the male principle.

Consequently, all the gods acquired consorts who were said to be incarnations of the Mahadevi. But to the masses, the Mother was still the Protector and the bestower of favours. The female deities came to be envisaged as the active and productive principle while the male gods were seen as passive and other-worldly. Their transcendence made them remote and too distant to concern themselves with daily existence. It was the Devi who was approachable and who could carry the messages of ordinary mortals to the gods – Parvati beseeches her husband to give up his meditation and attend to the prayers of his devotees. She can be worshipped in many forms – fierce as Durga and Kali or gentle and loving as Sita and Parvati.

Since creation was the prime activity of the Supreme Being, the male and female aspects came together as the *linga* and *yoni*, seen in the worship of Shiva. This embodies the union of the soul of the Universe, *Purusa*, with the primordial essence, *Prakriti*, representing nature.

Prakriti is the cosmic energy which manifests itself in the evolution of Nature while *Purusa* is the transcendent and changeless Spirit. *Prakriti* or *Shakti* when worshipped alone, is depicted as fierce, imbibing the energies of the gods to protect her devotees, but when worshipped with her consorts, she is seen as the peacemaker, gentle and amiable, in fact, the

Mother Goddess embodies paradox – she is gentle and fierce, beautiful and ugly, erotic and chaste.

Devi rules every aspect of life and so is often worshipped in groups like the *Saptamatrikas* (Seven Mothers) or the *Nav Durga* (Nine Durgas), yet all these are manifestations of the Great Goddess, Mahadevi.

The seven Mother Goddesses were created to vanquish the demon *Andhakasura*, who, besides his other evil deeds, once attempted to kidnap Parvati, Shiva's consort. Shiva's attempt to kill Andhaksura only resulted in several demons being born from each drop of his blood which touched the earth. Shiva then created Yogeshwari, who prevented the blood from falling to the ground. Seven of the gods, Brahma, Vishnu, Maheshwara (Shiva), Kaumara (a form of Vishnu), Varaha, Indra and Yama (Death), created their own Shaktis and sent them to assist Yogeshwari, thus destroying the demon.

These goddesses were the female forms of the gods and carried all the symbols associated with them as well as their names – Brahmani, Vaishnavi, Maheshwari, Kaumari, Varahini, Indrani and Chaumunda.

Brahma, Vishnu and Shiva may have reduced the power of the Devi as their consorts, but the two most powerful manifestations of the Mother Goddess – Durga and Kali – are still worshipped in their own right and form a cult of their own. In these incarnations the goddesses are not subservient to the gods and are themselves worshipped as the highest manifestation of the divine. The worship of Shakti is common among Tantric sects which generally have rituals embodying the fierce aspects of the female deities.

Whatever name she goes by and irrespective of her manifestations, she is the source of all things, the Universal Creator, "the form of Immensity". Combining both strength and gentleness, she stands at the very heart of creation and of Being. She is the enricher of mankind and the giver of supreme bliss.

Durga

Those who sing your praises with devotion and love,
Are not touched by sorrow and want.

~ Durga Chalisa

Dressed in red, a magnificent crown on her head, serene and beautiful, yet riding a lion, and carrying different weapons in her eight hands, Durga is the fiercer form of the gentle Parvati. The festival of Durga Puja or the *Nav Durgas* at *Navratri* (Nine Nights), in October, is celebrated with great extravagance and ceremony, specially in Bengal.

It is the return of Parvati to her father's home, away from the solitude of the Himalayas and her reclusive husband Shiva. She visits earth and is pampered by her devotees as a married daughter visiting her paternal home.

Images of the goddess are installed in public squares or in individual homes. For nine days she is the recipient of offerings in the form of food, clothes, flowers, even jewellery as families visit her to pay their respects. She is entertained with plays and musical performances, as she visits the illusory world of *maya* only once a year. On the 10th day she is given a tearful farewell and immersed in the waters of rivers or the ocean and helped on her journey back to Kailash.

Traces of the cult of Durga are found as early as the 1st century. AD, near Mathura. Later she evolved into Mahishasuramardini, the killer of the demon Mahishasura, and that image is still the most popular in all parts of India.

The demon Mahishasura posed a threat to

the gods because of the power earned through his penance. The gods appealed to Devi to subdue him. Brahma, Vishnu and Shiva combined the radiance of their heavenly countenances and created a most beautiful woman, and she gathered the energies and the weapons of all the gods and set out to confront Mahishasur. Interestingly, Durga, though a warrior fully armed, still retains the beautiful attributes of Parvati. Devi as Durga combined the energies of all the gods and collecting their weapons, the trident, the discus, the javelin and the sword, took nine days to fight and defeat him.

Mahishasura too changed his forms to mislead her till she slew him in the form of a buffalo, which ironically is considered a symbol of death. She is depicted standing, detached, with one foot on the buffalo with Mahishasura appearing out of it, and her vehicle, the lion, attacking Mahishasura from the rear.

With the death of Mahishasura, the cosmic equilibrium is regained and goodness reigns supreme. Durga is said to have assumed 10 forms or attributes to defeat a host of other demons. So, she is the ever-changing, elusive warrior. She is Durga – beyond reach. She is also said to have taken Krishna's place in his mother Devaki's womb as the seventh child, to save Krishna from being killed by his uncle, Kansa, and sacrificed her life for him, whereby she attained her place as one of the most important deities, as promised by Krishna.

The *Durga Chalisa*, a book with hymns dedicated to Durga, refers to her being reincarnated as all the female goddesses – Amba, Shakti, Annapoorna, Gauri, Saraswati. She is also the goddess Manasa, who protects against snake bites; Rati, the controller of love and sexual passions; Shasti, the divinity of childbirth and protectress of children, and Shitala, the deity of small-pox, who rides on an ass, searching for victims and thus has to be propitiated.

Kali

I bow to thee, leader of the realised, Noble Goddess who dwells in Heaven. I bow to you who are the auspicious Power of Time.

~ *Lord Krishna in the Mahabharata*

Kali is the female form of *Kala* or Time. She is the Origin and the End. As she represents the energy of Time, she is said to stand on the corpse of the Universe.

Her four arms mean absolute dominion over all that the world contains. Since she is Time, she is shown as a gaunt figure, wearing a necklace of skulls signifying that she supports the living and the dead.

She is black in colour, the ultimate energy in which all things disappear. Her terrifying image shows that she herself is without fear and thus can protect her worshippers from fear.

Like Shiva, she frequents lonely places like the outskirts of towns and even cremation grounds. In some myths, she is supposed to be the anger of Durga as she killed the demon Mahishasura. But the most popular myth depicts her as the killer of Raktajiva. As in the war with Mahishasura, each drop of blood from the evil Raktajiva produced new demons. Kali with the help of another form of Devi, Chandi, slew Raktajiva and was so overcome with her victory that she broke into a vigorous and ecstatic dance. The earth trembled and the heavens shook as the gods watched in helpless wonder.

Shiva stretched himself out on the firmament to contain her ecstasy, and Kali found herself standing over her husband. The true Hindu wife, she refrained

from putting her second foot down on her husband and in embarrassment stopped abruptly, her tongue hanging out in dismay. This story demonstrates that both are necessary to save the world from destruction – the male with his inertness and the female with her *shakti*.

Another account says that she sprang, in full armour, from the eye of Durga and joined her in destroying the powers of darkness.

Annapoorna

As Annapoorna, you are the sustainer of the world
You are the embodiment of Beauty.

Durga Chalisa

One of the most benevolent forms of the Devi is represented in Annapoorna, literally the deity of grain. She is the guardian deity of farmers and of their produce and those who worship her shall never go hungry.

As the Goddess of Plenty, she holds an overflowing pot of rice in one hand and a vessel brimming with milk in the other. She is a fair woman, sitting on a lotus or a throne, sometimes holding a large ladle resting on her knees.

There are several shrines dedicated to her in central and western India, where she is worshipped along with Shiva and Parvati.

But it is in Benaras that the most famous shrine is found. Since she is an incarnation of Shiva's

Gods & Goddesses

consort, she is said to have followed Shiva to Benaras when he retired there to expiate his sin of killing a Brahmin. She is said to have stayed there to provide food to Shiva as he wandered about seeking alms as a mendicant.

As Annapoorna, she so pleased Shiva by offering him food when he was hungry, that he is supposed to have embraced her so hard and with such force that they merged into one to become the *Ardhanarishwara* – the half-man half-woman form of Shiva.

Annakoot, the festival of Annapoorna in Benaras, literally stands for 'mountain of food'. This is the day when she is offered the 55 preparations of food, the *pachpan bhog*, which are then distributed as *prasad* (sanctified food) to the worshippers who throng her temple.

The Consorts Of The Gods

The Female Triad

पद्मासने स्थिने देवी, परब्रह्मस्वरूपिणी ।
सर्वदु : ख हरे देवि, महालक्ष्मी नमो स्तुते ॥

As Reality She is the power of co-ordination
As Consciousness She is the power of understanding
As Experience She is the power of delight
Sri Bhagwat Tattra

The Hindu Trinity – Brahma, Vishnu and Shiva – ruled the world as *brahmacharis* or bachelors, the second stage in the life of man. Their *shaktis* or energies, were within them waiting to be released at the appropriate moment. The time came as was ordained in Vaikunth, Vishnu's heaven.

The three gods had met to discuss the fate of Andhaka, the demon of darkness, who had the temerity to steal the Parijat tree from Swarga (heaven). As they were lost in thought, their glances met and held and their combined energies produced a brilliant female form. Each of the gods claimed her as his wife, so she divided herself into three and became the consort of all three gods – Saraswati, the White Goddess representing the Past and consort of Brahma, the Red Goddess, Lakshmi, the Present, consort of Vishnu, and Parvati, the Black Goddess, the Future, and consort of Shiva.

From then on, the Gods relied upon their consorts to assist them in their fight against evil. Each of the manifestations constituted a strong presence characterised by clearly identified attributes. Each deity was revered in both her individual as well as joint forms. Embodying virtue and strength, the consorts were irresistable beacons of light for the worshipping mind.

Saraswati

Brahma next formed from his immaculate substance,
a female called Saraswati.

~ *Matsya Purana*

 *Om* – the sound lingers on in the music and rhythm of the world, picked up on the strings of the *Veena*, held by the beautiful Saraswati, the Goddess of Learning. It is out of the *Om* that the universe was created by Brahma, Prajapati, Progenitor and consort of Saraswati.

According to other gods, she was incestuous, having been born out of the body of Brahma as the female principle of creation, and yet co-habiting with her father, thus playing both wife and daughter to Brahma. But she is also said to have emerged from Brahma's head and is known as the Manas Kanya, the child of the mind, and could be Brahma's Muse. She is addressed by other names, Satrupa, Savitri, Sati.

In the *Vedas*, she is essentially a river goddess. Nature worshippers, the Aryans deified rivers for their purity and fertility. But Saraswati, the mythical river which flowed from the Himalayas through the home of the Aryans, is now untraceable, having lost its way and petered out in the desert. And this time also, it was a curse which changed the course of its life. According to the *Mahabharata*, the sage Utathya cursed Varuna, the god of the waters for stealing his wife and caused all the rivers to dry up; Saraswati suffered the curse too. She has been identified with the rituals and hymns performed on the banks of the river, so she was called *Vach*, the goddess of speech and as such was believed to be the power behind all the celestial gods, since speech is the power through which knowledge is manifested.

The Aryans were supposed to have composed the first two *Vedas* on the banks of the Saraswati, hence she is known as the progenitor of the *Vedas*.

In the myths of the origin of the world, she was the instrument of creation. She is *saras*, the flowing one and represents the union of power and intelligence; the fluidity stands not only for water, but fluidity of speech and thought.

From Brahma, the Creator, were manifested the laws of the Universe, the *Vedas*. In the epic *Mahabharata*, Saraswati has also been called the Mother of the *Vedas* and the repositor of all Brahma's creative intelligence. With him she is the goddess of the creative and performing arts, and is recognized by the *Veena* she carries in her two hands.

Vach, speech, naturally presumes a storehouse of language, so Saraswati is also the inventor of the Devnagri script. She is *vidya*, knowledge, and as the goddess of eloquence and wisdom, she is often invoked as the Muse by poets and writers.

Poets, writers, musicians and even students pay obeisance to her, specially on *Basant Panchmi*, the spring festival. Yellow is the colour of spring, of re-awakening, and believers dye their clothes in this colour, extracted by boiling the stem of the *shefali* flower.

Saraswati is depicted as graceful, beautiful, riding on a peacock (or a swan) symbolising the ego, which must always be kept under control. In some icons, her vehicle is the swan which symbolises the sifting of true knowledge from life's experiences. In one hand she holds the rosary, emphasising the importance of prayer, and in the other a palm leaf scroll, showing that knowledge is man's sustenance. Dressed in white, she is Subhadra or the lady in white depicting the purity of true knowledge since the *vedic* tradition associated learning with white. She is supposed to give power and knowledge to her devotees and those she loves. On her brow is the cresent moon, identified with the essence of life, water.

It is interesting to note that her grace and serenity belie the stories told about her arrogance in the *Puranas*. The *Skanda Purana* tells of a *yagna* or sacrifice that Brahma was performing. The priest called for Saraswati, since all *yagnas* must be performed by a couple. She sent back a message to say that she was busy and would come later. As the auspicious time for the sacrifice was coming to an end, the furious Brahma ordered Indra to fetch the first woman he saw to be his wife. The perplexed Indra went out and saw a beautiful milkmaid, Gayatri, whom he persuaded to be Brahma's wife for the *yagna*.

When the sacrifice was over, Saraswati arrived and was furious to see another woman in her place. She pronounced a curse on all those who had been witness to this deed. Brahma was to be worshipped only once a year by mortals; Shiva was to be deprived of his manhood; Vishnu was to be born among mortals and lead the life of a nomadic cowherd. Lakshmi, his consort, would never be stationary and would live only among the sinful and the barbaric. The Brahmin priests who had presided over the ceremony were to perform sacrifices only for material gain.

The *Padma Purana* modifies this story and recounts how Savitri comes back at the entreaties of Vishnu and Lakshmi, is repentant and as befits a good wife, allows Gayatri to remain, provided she is subservient to Saraswati. Saraswati is even seen in Buddist sculptures as the consort of Manjushri, the Bodhisattva of Wisdom.

The image of Saraswati can be seen in temples dedicated to Vishnu and Ganesha perhaps because of her association with knowledge. When she is depicted with other gods, she appears standing, but when alone she is always seated.

The most beautiful sculptures of Saraswati are perhaps those at Halebid in Karnataka where she is shown as the *Nritta Saraswati* (or the dancing Saraswati), the goddess of dance and the performing arts.

Lakshmi

*Her, gods above and men below
As Beauty's Queen and Fortune know.*

~ Ramayana

Lakshmi, the consort of Vishnu, could not be separated from him for long. She was always with him, seated on *Seshnag*, at his feet, floating on the primeval water, or sitting on the lotus, the symbol of purity, or riding their vehicle Garuda. And yet the birth of Lakshmi, when she has been temporarily separated from Vishnu, and rises from the ocean of milk, is a spectacular description in the *Vishnu Purana*.

Due to the curse of a Brahmin, Durvasa, who felt he had been slighted by Indra, the kingdom of the gods lost its prosperity and energy. The *daityas* or demons, taking advantage of this, attacked the gods and defeated them in battle. The gods appealed to Brahma, who asked them to pray to Vishnu. Vishnu advised them to put all the medicinal herbs into the sea of milk and then churn it to extract *amrit* (ambrosia) from it.

The gods, churning the sea of milk to extract the ambrosia, by drinking which they could defeat the *asuras* or demons, saw among other things, a radiant beauty emerging from the water. She was seated on a lotus holding a water lily in her hand.

The gods and the sages were enraptured; the heavenly choir sang her praises and the celestial nymphs danced before her. The river Ganga and other holy rivers were her attendants and from vases of gold, the elephants of the sun poured water on her. The sea presented her with a crown of everlasting flowers and even Vishwakarma, the celestial artisan, adorned her

with beautiful ornaments. This beautiful maiden, turning away from the *daityas*, cast herself on Vishnu's breast, thus divesting the demons of prosperity and wealth, for she was wealth herself.

And yet, her separation from Vishnu came about due to an avaricious suggestion. Lakshmi, the daughter of Bhrigu, instigated her husband to ask for her part of her inheritance from her father. This so enraged Bhrigu that he cursed Vishnu to be born 10 times on earth and to be separated from his wife and have no children.

Despite the spirituality of Hinduism, prosperity and wealth are attributes to be taken seriously in the Hindu mind. Lakshmi, the Goddess of Good Fortune must be propitiated. Vishnu himself in the *Agastya Samhita* was supposed to have told Shiva to worship Lakshmi if he wished to have a vision of Rama, since Lakshmi was his innermost life and without her he could not exist for a moment. Thus every time Vishnu appeared in any of his incarnations, Lakshmi was born too. When Vishnu appeared in the *Vamana* or dwarf *avatar*, she was Padma, Kamala, born from the waters floating on a lotus; with Parasurama she was Dharini, the earth; Rama is never thought of without Sita, who was born when the earth was ploughed. She danced with Krishna in the forest of Vraj as Radha, or accompanied him to Dwarka as Rukmini. She was Jaladhija, ocean born and Lokmata, mother of the world.

The power of the all-pervading Vishnu is represented in the goddess of fortune – she of the Hundred Thousands. As the goddess of beauty she is Sri, and according to the *Taittiriya Samhita*, Beauty and Fortune are the two wives of the solar principle, Aditya. Both Lakshmi and Sri are found in the *Vedas*, associated with Fortune, but only in the epics is Fortune depicted as a major goddess. Beauty is also the mother of Kama or lust. She is known for her fidelity as a wife but as Fortune she is also known to be fickle.

Though associated with money and riches, she also signifies love and grace; she does not reside long with anyone who desires her only as wealth.

Lakshmi favours a beautiful, clean environment. Thus, during Diwali, when Lakshmi Puja is performed in most houses; the annual spring cleaning is done to prepare the house to receive the goddess.

The custom is to paint and clean the house. On the night of Diwali, after the lamps have been lit and the *puja* performed, the front door is left open to welcome her and make her passage easier.

Lakshmi is worshipped specially by the trading community, since they are beholden to her for their daily business. Lakshmi's elder sister Jyeshta, on the other hand, wallows in dirt and squalor, and the two sisters have a tacit understanding that they will never be together in the same place. Hence the ritual of cleaning up one's house to invite Lakshmi rather than Jyeshta!

There are several descriptions of Lakshmi. One text describes her as dark, while the *Amsumadbhedagama* says that she is of a golden colour, adorned with gold ornaments. Her beauty is so dazzling that all who look upon her love her. With her lotus eyes, a graceful neck and a beautiful form, she is a young girl on the threshold of womanhood. The *Shilpavatra*, a treatise on the arts, says that the colour of Lakshmi should be white.

Lakshmi, when seen with Vishnu, has only two arms, but when alone, there are four arms. The hands on the left hold the *amrit* vessel which she rescued from the ocean, and the conch shell which identifies her with Vishnu, and in the two right hands, a lotus and the *bilwa* fruit, called the *Sri-phala* or the fruit of fortune. Sometimes one hand is in the *abhaya mudra*, the gesture of fearlessness – the palm held up with fingers pointing upwards, while the other hand is in the *varada mudra*, bestowing grace and prosperity.

The red lotus she sits on signifies grace, love and peace and is also symbolic of the importance of pure living without which prosperity is dangerous. When Vishnu meekly allowed Bhrigu to kick him on the chest, Lakshmi felt insulted since she loved him, and angry with Vishnu for not retaliating, she left him and made her abode at Kolhapur in Maharashtra where she is even now worshipped as Mahalakshmi.

She left Vaikunth, but not before cursing Bhrigu and all Brahmins that they would be deprived of wealth and would live only by selling their knowledge. When Lakshmi left, she took the glory and wealth of Vaikunth with her, making the inhabitants very unhappy. So it was that Lakshmi came to reside on earth, and her devotees shower her with prayers and oblations to prevent her from leaving.

Parvati

*Shiva and Sati are as inseparable as cold from water,
heat from fire, smell from earth or radiance from the sun.*

~ Vaivarta Purana

Shiva and Sati (Parvati) are indeed seen as the eternal couple, who prayed to be together in all their reincarnations. In fact, inseparable, they are the ideal union of man and woman. In effect Parvati is recognized as being part of Shiva himself in his image as *Ardhnarishwara* or half-man half-woman.

Even to this day young girls see in Parvati the ideal wife who persevered against odds to have Shiva as her husband. They pray that through their penance and fasting on certain days set aside, like Gangaur in the state of Rajasthan, they would also be as successful as Parvati.

Parvati was first born as Sati or Uma, the daughter of Daksha and Prasuti. Even in her childhood she longed to be united with Shiva. She worshipped Shiva and thought only of him, and the god, all-knowing as he was, could not but be moved by her devotion, though he was hated by her father Daksha, who called him the impure and proud abolisher of rites. Daksha had the blessings of Brahma, who nominated him the keeper of custom and tradition and of law and authority. He was the chief of the Gods. In Daksha's world, nothing was allowed to disturb ancient custom and tradition. And 58 of his daughters adhered to it, but the youngest, the 59th, Sati, was different. Unimpressed with the pomp and ceremony of her father's court, she wandered in the forests and countryside in communion with nature. It was but natural that she should fall in love with the god Shiva, the ascetic, the Pashupati, Lord of Animals and Mountains. She married him against her father's wishes and was disowned by him. Mount Kailash became her home, and she shared all her husband's austerities, living under the open sky in summer, rains or winter, the true, ideal wife.

But she valued her independence, and displayed it to an astonished Shiva, when he requested her not to visit her father's house for the ritual sacrifice. Furious that her husband should forbid her, the mother of creation, she appeared before Shiva's awe-struck gaze in six of her manifestations; sometimes soft and feminine like Gauri; and at other times fierce and militant like Kali and Durga, so that Shiva had to acknowledge her superiority and let her go to her father's house, knowing full well that her father would not accept her as Shiva's wife. This foreboding was justified and due to the insults heaped upon her husband in his absence, Sati immolated herself in the sacrificial fire, and since then, a woman who burnt herself on her husband's funeral pyre came to be known as Sati, and was revered as a saint.

With Sati's death, Shiva was plunged into grief. He picked up her body and walked all over the universe, drying up rivers, withering plants and trees, causing death and destruction with his fury. The gods and mortals, fearing that Sati's death would bring the destruction of the world, appealed to Vishnu who descended to the earth and followed Shiva; to preserve the earth and all things in it, Vishnu fired 52 arrows at Sati's burnt body which fell in fragments all over the universe and wherever it fell, men recognizing it as something holy, built temples to the Mother Goddess. So the world was saved from being destroyed by Shiva, but Shiva himself gave up all pleasures and returned to his ascetic existence.

Unbeknown to him, Sita was reborn as Uma, Parvati, the daughter of Himmavat, the king of the Himalayas and his wife Menaka. In this birth too, Parvati was destined to marry Shiva, as from early childhood she brought offerings to his shrines, along with her sister, Ganga. And this time her earthly parents were on her side, being great devotees of Shiva.

But Shiva was oblivious of her rebirth and still grieved for Sati. It was then that Parvati performed penance, by fasting and prayer, to win Shiva. Following her example, millions of young girls offer prayers to Parvati, to grant them a husband with the qualities of Ishwar, or Shiva. It is said in the *Mahabharata* that even Rukmini prayed to her to have Lord Krishna as her husband, and succeeded.

But there are stories of their petty quarrels and misunderstandings. Parvati is now depicted as being golden in colour, but it is said that she was born dark, and one day Shiva angered her by calling her black. Insulted, she left him to perform austerities and prayed to Brahma, who granted her a boon, turning her into a dazzling gold, and she was then called Gauri, the golden one, and assured of her charms, she returned to Shiva.

Then again one day, Shiva caught her asleep while he was talking to her. When he accused her of slighting him, she denied it. Punishing her for her inattention and lies, he condemned her to fall to earth and live like a fisherwoman. But Shiva, who was inseparable from her, repented and sent his vehicle, Nandi the bull, to earth as a shark, which troubled the fisherfolk so much that they declared that the beautiful Parvati would be

Gods & Goddesses

married to the man who destroyed this shark. Shiva, who was waiting for this opportunity, descended to earth in the form of a fisherman and killed the shark, thus claiming Parvati and bringing her to Mount Kailash again.

Parvati is identified with the Great Goddess Devi. She is also the gentle goddess of light and beauty from whom the energy of the earth springs forth. Her father Himmavat represents the Ether, and her mother Menaka is Buddhi or intellect. She is benign and carries no weapon, and as Parvati has no cult of her own away from Shiva, the union of the two deities culminated in the image of Ardhnarishwara, where both Shiva and Parvati are combined, Parvati being on the left of Shiva. In some images the marriage of Shiva and Parvati is shown with Parvati sitting on his lap while he looks at her with tenderness, belying his usual image of Rudra or the terrifying one and showing his propensity for human emotions like love.

In her benign image she is the goddess of fertility and abundance, sometimes even identified with Annapoorna, the goddess of food. But though she is associated with Shiva as the *yoni* with the *linga*, the symbol of creation, she was destined never to be a natural mother due to the entreaties of the gods who felt that any child born of this union would be stronger and greater than any of the gods themselves. To allay their fears, Shiva promised that there would no such child, and Parvati was destined to be a mother only in name. Her son Ganesha was not the fruit of her womb, but rather of the rubbings from her body. But she was compensated by the great love and devotion he had for his mother, allowing his head to be cut off by Shiva rather than permit him to enter his mother's chamber.

Shiva and Parvati are shown very often with their sons Skanda or Kartikeya and Ganesha, a symbol of a happy family, an image not assigned to the other two gods of the Trinity.

Shiva as an ascetic is untouched by the pleas and prayers of his devotees, and it is only with the supplication of his wife that he attends to them and grants them boons and favours.

Sons Of The Gods

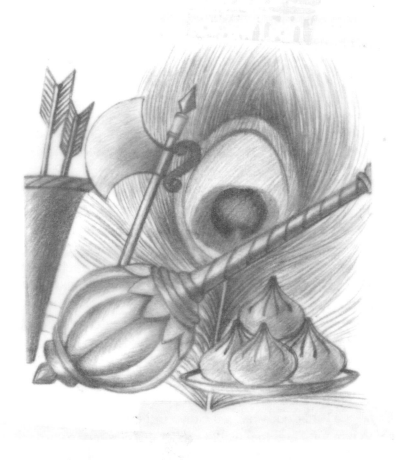

वक्रतुण्ड महाकाय सूर्यकोटिसमप्रभ ।
निर्विघनं कुरू मे देव सर्वकार्येषु सर्वदा ॥

Ganesha

*Praise be to thee Ganapati! Whoever meditates upon this figure,
never will be impeded by difficulties.*

~ *Ganapati Purana*

 Ganapati, Ganesha, Vinayaka – all ceremonies and rituals start with invocations to him. Marriages would not be 'made in heaven' if the festivities were not blessed by Ganesha. The occupancy of a new house, the inauguration of a new project or enterprise, the start of a journey, might be beset with problems unless Ganesha is propitiated.

Ganesha, the Elephant-God, son of Shiva and Parvati, is the god of wisdom and sagacity. He is also worshipped as the remover of obstacles that stand in the way of good deeds and actually plants obstacles in the path of evil activities. So the greater evils of life are removed through the working of the lesser evils.

According to the *Linga Purana*, the *asuras* or demons performed *pujas* and penance to propitiate Shiva, who, pleased with their prayers, granted them boons for strength and immortality, since a god has to reward those who call upon him.

Emboldened by Shiva's favours, they declared war upon the *devtas*. Indra and the other gods begged Shiva to have mercy on them and prayed to him for a god that would hinder the demons in carrying out their devotions to fruition. Shiva promised that since he could not punish the *asuras* himself, he would create a son out of his powers, who would be the Obstacle himself, as well as the Remover of Obstacles.

The *Shiva Purana* carries the story that is most common and known to most Hindus, a story that is told by grandmothers to their grandchildren to this day. Parvati was at her bath, and not wanting to be disturbed, she scraped the dirt off her body and fashioned a little boy out of it, infusing it with life. She ordered him to guard her door and forbade him to allow anyone to enter. Unfortunately, it was Shiva who arrived and was stopped at the gate by this boy. Impatient and impulsive as he always was, Shiva could not stomach this insult, so he cut off the boy's head. Parvati grieved for her lost son and would not be pacified till Shiva ordered the first head that could be found to be brought back and placed on Ganesha's trunk. This happened to be an elephant's head, which was fixed on to the boy's headless body.

Or take the story from the *Vaivartta Purana*, according to which, when a child was born to Shiva and Parvati, all the gods and *devtas* came to see the boy. Parvati, with a mother's pride, asked the god *Shani* (Saturn) to bless the boy, not realising that the god's brightness would burn the boy's head. Vishnu, it is said, mounted his vehicle Garuda and flew off to look for a substitute, and finding an elephant asleep on the banks of the river Pushpabhadra, took off his head and placed it on Ganesha's body. Ganesha was restored to life, but unfortunate Shani was cursed by Parvati and has limped ever since.

So, though neither human nor animal, Ganesha embodies the intelligence of Man's mind with the physical strength of an animal. He is considered the embodiment of supreme knowledge and divine wisdom.

He is also worshipped as the deity of the old, Jyeshtaraja, since he is particularly partial to them, beginning with his devotion to his parents. There is the story of how he and his brother Kartikeya challenged each other to see who could travel round the world first. While Kartikeya traversed the universe, Ganesha circled round his seated parents and declared that they were the world to him !

His fierce loyalty and respect are displayed by another story. Once Parasurama, the axe-bearing incarnation of Vishnu, came to visit his father Shiva. Ganesha would not let him pass, saying that his father was asleep. Whereupon, Parasurama tried to force his way, and the two came to blows. In anger, Parasurama hurled his axe at Ganesha, and Ganesha recognising it as the axe of his father, given as a gift to his favourite pupil, would not allow it to touch the ground and be contaminated, so he caught it on his tusk, thus breaking it, and earning the epithet of *Ekadanta* or the one-toothed.

There is another Puranic story regarding the broken tusk, which also shows his conscientiousness and his will to surmount any obstacle which stands in his way. Ganesha is said to be the writer of the *Mahabharata*, which was dictated to him by the sage Vyas. Ganesha, before taking up this task, stipulated that he would write it only if Vyas never faltered in his dictation and that what he dictated must be simple in meaning. While writing, his pen broke, but not wishing to interrupt the narrative, he calmly broke off the point of his tusk and continued to write. He is known to be learned and very well versed in the scriptures.

His large ears symbolise the fact that anyone who wishes to acquire knowledge should talk less and hear more; that is, he must be open to new ideas and opinions.

Ganesha himself is an easy-going, benevolent god. His round stomach symbolises patience and contentment, and that life should not get the better of one. All experience, whether good or bad, must be accepted equanimously. The stomach is the world and the serpent coiled around it is the energy which supports the universe.

Ganapati's vehicle is the apparently insignifigant mouse, signifying that a small body can still contain the infinite soul. It teaches man humility, since the soul or *atma* is the same in all living things.

A little mouse can destroy large structures and devour large stacks of grain. In the same way, man's greed and lust can be self-destructive. The mouse symbolises speed and the necessity for good, as against the large but slow moderation of the elephant.

Indirectly, the mouse symbolises Nature, a manifestation of *Shakti*, which emanates from

Shiva's wife and Ganesha's mother Parvati or Devi.

Though in some stories Ganesha is supposed to have two consorts, Siddhi and Buddhi, he is more often thought of as a *brahmachari* or bachelor. It is said that once, while playing with a female cat, he unwittingly hurt it. His anguish knew no bounds when he noticed the same scar on his mother Parvati's face and learnt that it was caused indirectly by him from the injury to the cat. As Parvati is the embodiment of the whole female world, any injury or humiliation to a female would have its repercussions on her. As a penance for this hurt, he decided to remain a bachelor all his life.

The worship of Ganapati has been known only since the 6th century AD since not much is written about him in the *Puranas*. The figure of Ganapati is said to have been derived from the symbol *Om*.

He was not a Vedic god but was perhaps a deity of the Dravadians. Interestingly, one of the oldest known images of Ganesha was found in the rock cut temples of Kung Hsien in China and is said to be from the early 6th century AD, perhaps because the Buddhists also seem to have adopted Ganesha. Ganapati is depicted in all the Shiva temples of Indonesia.

Ganapati was usually worshipped along with Shiva and Parvati and has acquired a special place in the Hindu pantheon only since Balgangadhar Tilak promoted Ganapati as a symbol of Hindu unity against the British and propagated the Ganapati festival in August-September in Maharashtra during which, every locality installs its own image of Ganapati and ritual *pujas* are performed every day for 10 days. This Ganesha festival is performed with lavish festivities to this day and Ganapati has become the *ishta devta* or personal god of most Maharashtrians.

The four arms of Ganapati symbolise the four *Vedas* or four castes which he has instituted. In one hand he holds the noose, to show that he will prevent evil influences from affecting his worshippers. One of his hands holds the driving hook. The third arm is in the *varada mudra*, showing him as the Giver and the fourth hand, in the *abhaya mudra*, allaying fears, assures mankind that he himself is beyond all fear because he has transcended the restraints of time and death, a condition which all mortals can strive towards in their redemption.

Kartikeya

Only the seed of Shiva can produce a hero
who will defeat the powers of evil.

~ Kumara - Sambhava

Such a seed was Kartikeya, the son of Shiva, but born without the medium of a female. Again it was a tale of demons and boons, love and devotion. For *Skanda*, as Kartikeya was called, was created just to destroy the demon Taraka. Unwittingly, Brahma had granted his demon devotee Taraka, a boon which assured him immortality. Taraka had been practising austerities for over a 100 years, burying himself in earth, immersing himself in water, and enduring burning fires on his body. And the boon was that he could be killed only by a son of Shiva. But Shiva had been living a life of abstinence for a 1000 years, since his beloved wife, Sati, had consigned her physical body to the sacrificial fire when her father Daksha had cast aspersions on her husband, Shiva. When gods and mortals prayed to Brahma to free them from Taraka's evil exploits, Brahma sent Kama, the god of love, to arouse Shiva from his prayers and unite him with his wife, since Sati had been reborn as Parvati and had been searching for her husband. After several tribulations, including the slaying of Kama by Shiva, Parvati and Shiva were reunited. But for a long time there was no child born to them. In despair, Agni visited Shiva at a time when Shiva had just left his wife, and was still full of desire. Agni was chosen to carry the seed of Shiva to be nurtured and borne away from the father. Assuming the form of a dove, Agni sped away, but was not strong enough to carry the seed of the great god, so he dropped it into the Ganga. The egg lay on the banks of the sacred river, which nurtured it till it was time for its emergence and from it was born a boy as beautiful as the moon and as bright as the sun. As he lay there, he was seen by six princesses who used to bathe in the river. Struck by his beauty, each claimed him for her son, and to please them all, Kartikeya developed six heads so that he could be nursed by them all, so he came to be known as *Shanmukha*, the six-headed. His six heads symbolise the five senses and the mind which if working together, symbolise spiritual growth.

Kartikeya was also created by Brahma on the plea of Indra. The *Mahabharata* recounts the story of how once when the *danavas* or demons had gained supremacy over the *devtas* or gods, Indra had encountered a woman in the forest. Her name was Devasena, and she was the army of the gods, but her strength had been destroyed by her sister Daityasena, the army of the demons. Devasena begged Indra to find her a strong husband since she could no longer outwit the demons on her own strength. Indra convinced Brahma that it was in the interest of the gods that Devasena be granted her wish. Thus, Brahma ingeniously manipulated that Agni, the ritual fire, should father a son through Swaha, a daughter of Daksha. Since Agni is identified with Rudra and thus Shiva, and Swaha, being mentioned as a daughter of Daksha, is also Shiva's father-in-law, by a complicated turn of manifestations and incarnations, Kartikeya is recognised as the son of Shiva and Parvati.

In all the stories about his birth, Kartikeya was said to be born only of a father, Shiva and did not have a natural mother. There is another story of how Shiva's bright eyes emitted such strong sparks that they fell into the lake Saravana and from them were born six infants. When Parvati saw these children she was so ecstatic that she embraced them so hard altogether that their bodies became one but their six heads and 12 arms remained.

Kartikeya married Devasena and defeated Taraka in battle and has since been known as the deity of war, the general of the celestial army. His symbol is a peacock, a symbol of pride and egotism kept under control by the *yogi*. In his hand he carries a pointed spear, signifying the sharpness of the intellect.

The strength of Kartikeya is legendary and he even dared to challenge Vishnu to pull out his spear which he had thrust into the earth. He is depicted as an extremely handsome man dressed in red clothes, holding a large bow in his hands.

Kartikeya is worshipped more in the south, where he is known as Shanmugha, Murugan, Subramanya or Kumara, and there are several temples dedicated to him. In the north, there are no temples for him and in fact, he is viewed as inauspicious for women, since any female casting a glance at him is doomed to widowhood. Perhaps because he is generally believed to be a bachelor, and prejudiced against women, he has no women devotees. His only wife is Devasena, who is probably a personification of the celestial army and not a woman at all.

The name of Skanda appears even in ancient texts such as those of Patanjali. Worshipped in the north during the Gupta period (4 - 7 AD), Kartikeya is now worshipped almost exclusively in the south where the most famous of his temples are situated. However, Kartikeya is also the hero of *Kumarasambhavam,* a literary work by Kalidasa, the great Sanskrit poet. A figure to gladden the heart, Kartikeya is completely devoted to his parents.

Hanuman

Hail Hanuman, as dear to me as Bharat, my brother.

~ Lord Rama in the Ramayana

Hanuman, the chief of the monkey army of Rama, has a large following of worshippers. He is known as the embodiment of the devotion that Hindus have for Rama. His selfless dedication to Rama and his exiled family, forms a large part of the *Ramayana* and he is worshipped as the main god in several villages of north India. Tuesday is the day set aside for the worship of Hanuman, when his followers fast and visit his temple to propitiate him with offerings. Shrines to Hanuman are put up by the roadside or in fields, wherein he is usually painted orange and is depicted carrying the mountain on which grows the *sanjivani* (life-giving) plant. Besides his agility and speed, he is also credited with immense knowledge and even Rama extols this aspect of his. "For his long speech how well he spoke ! In all its length no rule he broke." (*Ramayana* i tr. Griffith)

Monkeys swarm many temples in India and feeding them is seen as a meritorious act, since they are thought of as the representatives of Hanuman. Causing them injury or death is an unpardonable sin which no Hindu wishes to be guilty of.

The God of Wind, Vayu, once saw Anjana, an *apsara* (celestial being), who had been condemned to live in the form of a monkey queen due to a curse. Vayu was infatuated with her, and as was ordained, fathered a son, Hanuman, by her. It is said in another story that Anjana gave birth to Hanuman after swallowing a rice cake meant for Kaikeyi, Rama's step-mother. Hanuman's birth had been planned to coincide with Rama's on earth, since Hanuman was to be the leader of Rama's army against Ravana, the king of Lanka.

Hanuman, even as a child, displayed great courage and ability. Seeing the sun in the sky, he leapt up and tried to eat it, mistaking it for something edible. The sun took flight and Hanuman followed it till he reached Indra's abode. Alarmed, Indra hit him with a bolt, thus damaging his cheek and face and earning him in history the name of Hanuman or the 'long-jawed one'. Vayu, his father, taking revenge on the gods, caused the breeze to remain stagnant, thus depriving the world of life-giving air. The gods came to appease him and Brahma blessed Hanuman with immortality in battle while Indra apologised and swore never to harm him in future. It is said that the sun, in surrender, bestowed upon him golden clothing which could only be seen by Rama and so identify his devotee to him.

Thus fortified, Hanuman joined the forces of Rama as he went forth to rescue Sita from the clutches of the demon Ravana.

Hanuman's ability to alter his size and to make himself invisible gave him an advantage over the other monkeys, and Rama choose him to visit Lanka surreptitiously, both to carry his message to Sita and reassure her that she would be rescued and also to study the lay of the land. Hanuman was said to have retired to the mountains both to meditate and to gather his strength. As he prayed, his body grew in size till he was larger than the mountain. Assured of his might, he took flight, carried by his father Vayu, and after many adventures, arrived at Ashoka Vatika, the garden where Sita was imprisoned. The story of Hanuman's first meeting with Sita, whom he revered as his mother and the presenting of Rama's ring to her for his identification as Rama's messanger, form some of the most poignant verses of the epic, *Ramayana*. The tale is told and retold endlessly in every hamlet, town and city of India.

Lanka witnessed the fury of Hanuman soon after, as with his blazing tail set afire after being captured by Ravana, he broke his fetters and set fire to the whole kingdom.

Hanuman was always by Rama's side during the battle with Ravana. He is said to have carried Rama on his shoulders while crossing the sea to Lanka. Led by Hanuman, the army of monkeys went onto the battlefield, carrying uprooted mountains as weapons, causing disarray in the ranks of the *rakshasas*. The wily Ravana, using his powers of illusion, created several forms of Hanuman who surrounded Rama belligerently. Rama the god, all-knowing and all-powerful, dispelled these illusory animals and led the attack against Ravana himself.

A very common depiction of Hanuman appears with him flying across the continent, carrying a mountain balanced on his palm. Lakshmana, Rama's devoted brother, was wounded in battle and on the point of death; the only thing that could save him was the *sanjivani* plant that grew on the Himalaya mountains. Hanuman promptly rushed from Lanka to the other end of the country and not being able to recognise the plant, in his impatience uprooted the whole mountain and bore it across the sky to restore Lakshmana to life. He had to face several obstacles and onslaughts before he could retrieve the herbal plant and carry it back to Lanka. Kalameni, Ravana's uncle, went to the Himalayas disguised as a devotee and tried to poison Hanuman; but Hanuman being warned against him by an *apsara* he had rescued from a curse, took him by his feet and hurled him all the way to Lanka. Rama and Lakshmana were saved by this medicinal plant, and to this day, the *sanjivani* plant found in the heights of the Himalayas, is still used in ayurvedic medicines.

Hanuman is the deity of strength, vitality and energy. Known as Mahavira or the Great Brave, he is worshipped by soldiers, sportsmen and all those who pray for strength of body and mind. His devotion to Rama earned him eternal youth and immortality, and he is pictured parting his chest to show his heart on which there is an imprint of his overlord, Rama and his wife, Sita.

It is interesting to note that certain scholars consider Hanuman and his monkey army to have been members of an ancient tribe of totemic people who took their name and identify from the monkey.

All Things Holy

यो विद्यात् सूत्रं विततं यस्मिन्नोता : प्रजा इमा :।
सूत्रं सूत्रस्य यो विद्यात् स विद्याद् ब्राह्मणं महत्

We bow to you as vegetal life, by which the world subsists and which —
six in kind, trees, creepers, bushes, plants, herbs and bamboo — supports
the sacrificial rites.
We bow to your serpent shapes, lustful and cruel, whose forked
tongues know no mercy.
~ Vishnu Purana
The All-Powerful Divinity dwells as the living individuality in all
living things. Hence the wise bows before a horse, a cow or an ass.
~ Yajnavalkya Upanishad

 And so the Hindu respects everything that has an effect on life. All forms of life are sacred and cannot be ignored in daily worship. Trees, rivers, professional implements, animals and birds are either worshipped in connection with one of the gods or as individual deities. Since, as we have seen, gods often take on animal *avatars*, it was safer to treat all animals with respect in case one unknowingly offended the reincarnated deity. According to their belief in the transmigration of souls, one could be reincarnated in any form according to one's *karma*.

Every animal directly or indirectly has some connection with one of the myths or is associated with the gods – the elephant with Lakshmi, the swan with Saraswati, Garuda with Vishnu, the mouse with Ganesha, the bull with Shiva, the cow with Krishna – the list is endless. Religion saw the need for an equilibrium in the universe and ecology and environment were protected by these norms.

Trees and plants were the most visible manifestations of Prakriti or Nature, which is identified with the Mother Goddess. The planting of a tree is considered a sacred act and watering and nurturing it ensures you merit in heaven.

The most sacred of plants is the *tulsi*, which in effect is said to be the

wife of Vishnu. It is said that Tulsi was a woman who
prayed for centuries in the hope of marrying Vishnu.
Lakshmi, fearing a rival in Tulsi, turned her into a plant.
But Vishnu, impressed with her devotion, assumed the form of
shaligram (ammonite) and vowed to live close to the *tulsi* plant for
eternity.

Another myth connects Tulsi with Lakshmi who is born as Radha
at the time of the Krishna incarnation and since Radha could not
marry Krishna in this incarnation, the *tulsi* plant is united symbolically
to him. The marriage of Tulsi with Krishna is still celebrated sometime
in November, specially in the temples of Mathura.

The *tulsi* is planted in the courtyards of most Hindu households. Since
she was not Krishna's legitimate wife, she could not cross the threshhold.
She is the personification of wifely devotion and sacrifice. The women
of the household pray to Tulsi, offering it water and flowers. The *tulsi* leaf
is an essential part of any offering made to the gods, specially in the
pujas to any of the worshipped incarnations of Vishnu.

One of the first things created by Brahma is said to be the *bael* or
wood apple tree. This tree is sacred to Shiva and is found near Shiva
temples, the leaves and fruit being offered daily to the deity. The *bael*
leaf resembles Shiva's trident in its formation. A story relates how a
hunter, while taking refuge on a *bael* tree, unknowingly plucked the
leaves and let them fall on a shrine of Shiva which had been built
under the tree. Shiva was so pleased with this offering that he blessed
the hunter and gave him the fruits of heaven even though the hunter
was a non-believer.

It is also considered the abode of Lakshmi, and during the festival
of Durga Puja in Bengal, the goddess Durga is invited to take up her
residence in the tree during the duration of the festival, perhaps because
of its association with Shiva. The *bael* tree is believed to grant success
in various endeavours, and like Ganesha, it is also
worshipped before the start of new ventures.

The banyan tree is said to be chosen by God

to weather any storm, even that of *pralaya*, the destruction of the world. In the last deluge, one leaf of the tree was carried by the primeval waters till the universe was recreated by God, and the tree began an existence in another cosmic age, so the tree has also been associated with immortality. As such, it is specially worshipped by married women who recall the story of Savitri and Satyavan and worship the tree on *Vad Purnima*, the day of the full moon in June. There is a symbolic marriage with the tree because it is said to guarantee a long and happy married life to those who pray to it. Savitri is the epitomal wife who followed Yama, the god of death, to the gates of his kingdom to rescue her dead husband from him. Yama, impressed by her perseverance, restored her husband to life under the banyan tree.

The banyan tree is also associated with fortune and wealth, since Lakshmi, the Goddess of Wealth, is said to visit it on Sundays.

Ficus religiosa, even the botanical name of the *peepal* tree, suggests its sacred character. It is perhaps the oldest tree mentioned in legends and myths and has been venerated for centuries. It is believed that its root is Brahma, and the stem, Vishnu, and nearly every deity of the Hindu pantheon has been associated with it. Destruction of this tree brings down the wrath of the gods. The Buddhists also venerate this tree, since the Buddha was said to have gained enlightenment under its branches,and in Buddhist lore it is known as the Bodhi Tree, or the Tree of Knowledge.

As the gods churned the ocean for *amrit*, the third object that emerged out of the waters was the *parijat* tree, the Queen of the Night and "the delight of the nymphs of heaven, perfuming the world with its blossoms". Indra, the God of the Sky, deeming it too beautiful for the earth, carried it to the heavenly garden of Amravati. But it was brought back to earth by Krishna, who was cajoled into carrying it back by his wife, Satyabhama. It flourished in Krishna's garden and came to be regarded as the celestial tree, its flowers being offered in the *puja* or ritual worship.

Perhaps the flower most seen in images and representations of the Hindu gods is the lotus. Vishnu waited, reclining on it, when the world was in the process of creation. Brahma appeared on a lotus which grew out of Vishnu's navel. Lakshmi, Vishnu's consort, is called Padmini or Kamala (of the lotus) and she sits on the lotus flower. Saraswati, the Goddess of Learning, Ganesha, the son of Shiva and Parvati – in fact, most of the Hindu deities have lotus pedestals or thrones. The lotus in Hindu thought represents the world as also the *atma* (soul) of man which is the dwelling-place of God. In the *Vishnu Purana*, the Lord is invoked as "Dweller in the lotus of the heart". The lotus also symbolises purity, since it remains undefiled by its surroundings, an example for mortals, teaching them that they should live untouched by the evil and impurities around them. The lotus has thus become associated with beauty, purity and prosperity and is one of the important symbols of the Hindu religion.

It is quite usual for a devout Hindu to keep aside the first three morsels from his major meals of the day for the cow, a dog and a crow.

Each form of life has its special niche in the universe and has always been considered essential for the balance of nature. Different animals are venerated in different parts of India. The dog, the vehicle of a local deity, Bhaironji, in western India; the mouse, the vehicle of the god Ganesha; the peacock, associated with Kartikeya; the swan with Saraswati; the serpent Sheshnag with Vishnu. Shiva in his role of Pashupati, the Lord of the Beasts, is seen surrounded by various animals.

But it is the cow which has a special place in the Hindu reverence of animals. It is said that the first thing to come out of the ocean of milk was *Surabhi*, the Cow of Plenty. She is "the fountain of milk and curd, worshipped by the divinities "; she was also the sacred wish-fulfilling cow, *Kamadhenu*. Shes belonged to the sage Jamdagni and was supposed to have fed the whole army of Kartavirya not with milk only, but with food to suit each taste. Being the provider, the cow was seen as the mother, *gaumata*, giving life and sustaining food to infants and adults alike.

In later Hinduism, with the worship of Krishna who lived among the cowherds, the Yadavs, the cow took on a greater significance, and new legends grew around the cow. Krishna grew up on milk, was accused of stealing curd and butter by the *gopis* or milk-maids; when he played on his flute, the cows would gather round him and sway to the music in ecstasy, very much like his devotees who would lose themselves in the devotional songs that are composed and sung about the life of Krishna. It is believed that even now, the cow carries a reflection of Krishna in its eyes.

A common sight is that of cows being tethered at temple entrances and at well-frequented corners, and passers-by reverentially touch the animal or feed it with bundles of grass that can be bought from the attendants at a small price.

The serpent in Hindu thought symbolises the energy essential for spiritual conquest, and thus it is seen in the representations of most of the Hindu gods. Semi-divine mythical beings called *Nagas*, are shown with human faces but the tails of serpents. One of the daughters of these *Nagas* was said to have given birth to the entire *vanar sena* or the army of the monkeys which helped Rama to defeat Ravana, the demon king in the epic *Ramayana*. This gave the serpents a special place in the hierarchy of divine beings. Snakes are seen in the representations of several gods – Shiva wears snakes coiled round his throat and hair, Ganesha has a snake as a girdle, Vishnu and Lakshmi are seated on the coiled *Sheshnag*, who is a symbol of eternity, and he also forms a canopy over Vishnu with a thousand heads. Krishna is seen dancing on the hood of Kalia, who, along with his wives, became his devotees.

The king of serpents, Vasuki, was used by the gods as a rope to churn the ocean for nectar. Manasa, the Goddess of Serpents, was believed to be the daughter of Shiva and the sister of Sheshnag and she is worshipped today since she is still supposed to cure snakebite by drawing out the venom of snakes. Sheshnag himself is said to have been persuaded by Brahma to support the earth and hence has to be propitiated to maintain the balance on earth. Nagas are also believed to be the spirits of trees and rivers, and their worship is probably a continuation of the Dravidian snake cult. Today, snakes are worshipped on the festival of *Nag Panchmi*, which falls sometime in August. Snake charmers go into the forests to persuade the *nag devtas* or snake gods, to come out of their hideouts to accept the offerings of mortals, consisting of rice and milk. Snakes are also taken out in processions which end at the local shrines of Shiva, the Lord of Beasts.

There are several other animals which are considered sacred and are protected by believers. The mouse, the vehicle of Ganesha, is specially protected in a temple dedicated to *Karni Mata*, a form of the Devi, at Bikaner, in the state of Rajasthan. Durga rides a lion and is known as *Simha Vahini* or *Simha Rathi* (the lion borne). Shiva sets his foot on a lion as he climbs on his mount, *Nandi*. The tiger is the vehicle of *Shakti*, the symbol of *prakriti* or nature. Jatayu, "a mighty vulture of size and strength unparalleled", offered to protect Sita when she was left alone in the forest.

The animal and mortal world interacted with each other and often was the link between man and his gods, thereby gaining an assurance of safety and sanctity from the depradations of the human world.

Epilogue
The Undefinable

Who really knows, who could here proclaim,
Whence this Creation flows, where is its origin
With this great surge the Gods made their appearance
Who therefore knows from where it did arise ?

~ Rig Veda

Ekam eva advitiyam (There is but one Being, only one). This thought is expressed in the most sacred of syllables, the *Om*, which is chanted at the beginning and end of all Hindu rituals and prayers. The Hindu prays to his own individual deity, at the same time never forgetting that though he worships the aspects of divinity in its diverse forms, these are only a support through which he reaches the Principle. When he shuts his eyes in *dhyana* or meditation it is this Absolute that he is searching for in his concentration. This is the pure Brahman who is beyond quality, beyond form or attributes – the *Nirguna* Brahman.

It was this Brahman to whom even Brahma, the Creator was said to have prayed for knowledge to create a new world. This Absolute was immanent, all around us, within us and in all things that had been manifested in the world. Hinduism recognises the highest state of man as that in which the Unbounded Consciousness is perceived in everything,and it is this state which is the ultimate goal of all spiritual endeavour.

The concern of every Hindu is *moksha*, the union of the *atman* (soul) with the Brahman or Supreme Spirit, and he strives to achieve it knowing that it is the ordeal of *karma* and rebirth which he has to surmount through his *dharma* or right action. So he tries to go from the gross to the transcendental, never losing sight of his ultimate goal.

The believer knows that it is extremely difficult to grasp this Immensity, this casual, formless, all-pervading divinity, the Unknown beyond which his comprehension cannot go.The gods and goddesses help him in his journey through the material world, which in any case is *maya* (illusion); they are predictable, their reactions known and understood and they could be propitiated. But of the Brahman one knows nothing. It surpasses definition. So the Hindu chose the sacred symbol *Om*, the concentrated chanting of which is said to release vibrations and an energy which connects him to the Supreme Energy, the source of all creation in the universe. Life in all its forms sprang from this Energy, the Universal Spirit and all things merge with it, losing their individual entity.

So Man (*atman*) and Brahman (Spirit) are destined to become one and all images of man, animal or gods are but illusions or *maya* in this *lila* (divine play) of the Supreme Consciousness. For as the *Bhagvata Gita* says of God, "Do not think of me as the Creator of this and other worlds, for I am changeless and create nothing."

Suggested Reading

Hindu Mythology	Kennedy
Elements of Hindu Iconography	I. A. Gopinath Rao
Hindu Fasts and Feasts	Abhay Charan Mukerji
Hindu Gods and Goddesses	H. A. Rose
The Splendour of Worship	Laxmi Tiwari
The Hindu God Universal	K. Narayanaswami Aiyar
Vaishnavism, Saivism, and Other Minor Religious Systems	R.G. Bhandarkar
Dravidian Gods in Modern Hinduism *The Christian Literature Society for India*	Elmore Wit
Tree and Serpent Worship	J. Fergusson
Gods and Men	G. S. Ghurye
Hindu Mythology	W. J. Wilkins
Insights into Hinduism	R. N. Dandekar
Vishnu and His Incarnations	Shakti Gupta
From Daityas to Devtas in Hindu Mythology	Shakti M. Gupta
Vishnu Purana Punthi Pustak *Vishnu Sahasranama*	Tr. by H.H Wilson
Iconography of the Hindus,Buddhists and Jains	R. S. Gupte